Daddy's Home

Daddy's Home

Mike Clary

Seaview Books

NEW YORK

Copyright © 1982 by Mike Clary.

All rights reserved. No part of this book may be reproduced, stored in a retrieval system, or transmitted in any form by an electronic, mechanical, photocopying, recording means or otherwise, without prior written permission of the author.

Manufactured in the United States of America.
First edition.
Seaview Books/A Division of PEI Books, Inc.

Library of Congress Cataloging in Publication Data
Clary, Mike.
    Daddy's home.
    1. Clary, Mike. 2. Fathers—Michigan.
3. Infants (Newborn)—Michigan. 4. Father and child.
I. Title
HQ756.C54   306.8'7   81-52067
ISBN 0-87223-746-X   AACR2

---

for Lillian

Contents

	Acknowledgments	ix
1.	Just a Baby, Only a Man	3
2.	The Domestic Pioneer	23
3.	Childcare Mechanics	41
4.	Love and Homemade Adventure	50
5.	The Baby Mixer	64
6.	A Gently Terrific Birth	77
7.	Our Child, Our Responsibility	88
8.	The Inverted Macho of the Househusband	103
9.	The Only Man in the Park	111
10.	The Father as Son	124
11.	A Man's Game	130
12.	The Blue-Mood Special	138
13.	Like Any Other Mother	156
14.	The Sneakers' Lament	170

CONTENTS

15.	*Fear and Surgery*	*178*
16.	*The Classroom Carnival*	*191*
17.	*The She-Bear in Me*	*201*
18.	*Hot News and Cool*	*209*
	Epilogue	*223*

Acknowledgments

THIS BOOK began as a letter. Of those who responded to my epistolary questions and confessions, I am especially grateful to my parents, Lillian's parents, Nan Durbin and Dorothy Santo Hattem. Along the way I benefited from advice offered by Lary Bloom, Doug Balz, Madeleine Blais, and Jim Ricci. I was sustained by the counsel and confidence of my editor, Sherry Huber. Fast, precise typing, and suggestions, were provided by Doris Gallagher and Barbara Sciandra. For room to work I am indebted to Mike and Betsy Castner, and the Rev. Howard Gordon and the Riviera Presbyterian Church of South Miami. Without two people, of course, there would have been no book. Lillian never tired of reading just one more draft, of asking me to go a little further, of keeping me honest. And Annie was there, my daughter, my muse.

Many of the names in this book have been changed. There is, for example, no Bexley College. But there is in Michigan a small college town filled with people very much like the ones described here. The story is true.

Daddy's Home

Chapter 1

Just a Baby, Only a Man

ANNIE woke up howling. I hunched further down in the bed, burrowed deeper into the pillow, and kept my eyes closed. Perhaps I was dreaming. Perhaps she would stop. Perhaps a local radio station was about to call and ask me Willie Mays's lifetime batting average.

"Willie Mays," I would repeat through the fog, stalling, hurrying to wake up, hopeful that a baseball statistic of such significance was somewhere in my head. "Uh, Willie Mays's average . . . was that, uh, .302?"

"Congratulations, sir! You have just won a full week's worth of *total childcare,* plus complimentary *floor-to-ceiling housecleaning,* from Rear Enders, the designer diapers that

DADDY'S HOME

fit tight. So relax. Because Miss Prudence Golightly, a registered, professional nanny, will be right over. And you have yourself a real nice day, you hear?"

You mean, I really wouldn't start my full-time job as a househusband today? I really wouldn't have to take care of Annie all by myself after Lillian left for work? You mean, I really *could* sleep in?

Through the crying I listened for the phone. It didn't ring. Time was running out. A million years of evolution had honed Annie's wail to an intensity that, at close range, was beyond parental bearing. The bassinet was at the foot of the bed. I could not outwait the baby.

But deep in my cocoon of blankets and fatigue, I thought I might be able to outwait Lillian. She lay motionless next to me. I suspected she was playing possum, too. If she acknowledged the cry before I did, then she would have to get up and answer it. That seemed only fair. I had been up half the night with Annie, coaxing her back to sleep. I was too tired to get up again.

I waited for Lillian to move.

"Mike?"

Aha! I knew this gambit: the straightforward approach. She admitted hearing the cry, but was going to ask me to respond. It was just like her to confound my games with honesty and deal with reality head-on.

I decided not to acknowledge Lillian, either.

"Mike?" She put a hand on my shoulder.

I was sleeping; couldn't she see that?

"Mike." She gave my shoulder a slight nudge.

I was too exhausted to even answer; couldn't she sense that?

"Mike!" she said quite loudly, rocking me.

"What?" I mumbled peevishly.

"Can you get Annie and bring her here?"

Just a Baby, Only a Man

"What time is it?" I asked, as if that mattered.

Lillian turned toward the clock, and I grabbed for the retreating covers.

"Seven-thirty."

"I just got to sleep," I whined.

"You exaggerate. You've been in bed since four."

"I *feel* like I just got to sleep."

"You've got to get up anyway. And I want to nurse her here in bed."

Slowly I struggled to a sitting position. Rubbing my forehead to loosen my eyes, I wondered if there was another man anywhere who had volunteered to get up so often to take on a job for which he had so little preparation. Just what was it I had gotten myself into?

The window beside the bed was filled with pale blue sky. It was a Monday in early September in a small college town in the geographic center of Michigan's lower peninsula, and I was about to put in my first full day as a housespouse. At the age of thirty-four, after twelve years of newspaper reporting that had taken me from covering killer tornadoes in Ohio to rock festivals in London to aborigine uprisings in Australia, I was about to begin the biggest assignment of my life: raising Annie, the thirteen-day-old girl squalling at my feet.

All I had to do was look after her for the next two years. But when the bell sounded to begin, I did not feel ready.

"Oooooouunaaagh!" I snorted, urging myself on.

"You can do it," Lillian cheered.

Swinging my legs over the side of the bed, I stared at a blister on my toe, a memento of a three-set tennis match with my friend Roger Vander the day before. Even my feet looked limp.

As tired as I felt, I tried to remember that Lillian was even more tired. Annie's birth had been a grueling odyssey, a wrenching ordeal that had drained her and left her flat. After a full day of nagging, dilatory labor, Lillian had gamely hung on through almost four hours in the delivery room, pushing through unexpected pain and blood, through my flare-ups of anxiety. Our physician, Jim Howard, had called the birth the toughest he had been in on in years. Annie's arrival bore little resemblance to the easy sublimity for which our Lamaze training had prepared us. For Lillian, still held together with stitches, climbing the stairs was an act of courage.

Over the horizon of a green blanket, a tiny fist made agitated circles in the still morning air. Heaving myself from bed, I bent to confront a face crimson with exertion.

"What do I have to do to get some sleep around here? How come you don't tire like I do?"

Her cry rolled on, like waves.

Lillian opened a pocket for her under the covers, and after another few seconds of shrill defiance, Annie eased into a noisy moan of satisfaction.

I picked up my pants, coiled on the floor where I had dropped them, and stumbled into them.

"How do you feel?" I asked Lillian.

"I can't tell yet," she said quizzically. "All right, I think."

"Maybe you're not ready to go back to work yet."

"If I wait until I'm ready, I might never go back." She smiled.

I looked at mother and child. Nestled at Lillian's side, Annie seemed too small to be capable of the racket she made. But students had told me that from the union across the street they had heard her cries between records on the jukebox. I could hear her whimpers from anywhere in the house. My newfound acuity amazed me. Before becoming a father, I had been able to sleep through anything—roistering fraternity brothers in the street, Katydog's barking, the

Just a Baby, Only a Man

fire alarm in the boardinghouse next door. Now I had rabbit ears. Even Annie's sighs sounded reveille in my brain, and I was blasted awake at least three times a night. It was like being in the army, but worse. In boot camp, I'd collapsed into sleep knowing that Drill Sergeant Mendoza's dread call, "UPANATUM, NUMBNUTS!," would come at 5:30, like an air raid. His voice was a nightmare, but the nightmare was scheduled.

Annie's intrusions were random, and, ever on call, waiting to be rousted, I couldn't settle into the black unconsciousness I associated with true restfulness. Each time I woke up, I felt like I had been dozing. A slight ache lurked behind my eyes; my legs felt heavy. Eventually, I figured a wispy tiredness was part of the baggage that comes with a child; and through those first weeks after Annie's arrival, I hauled that feeling around like a cross.

My path downstairs to the kitchen was strewn with evidence of our dance with sleeplessness only hours before: three sticky receiving blankets; an unrinsed, ripening diaper; assorted rattles; a never-used pacifier; a half-empty bottle of sterilized water; four record-album jackets, indicating lullaby attempts ranging from Handel's "Water Music" to *The Who, Live at Leeds*. What a martyr I became at three in the morning when Annie turned tiny terrorist and held me hostage in the living room with her menacing threat of explosion. Cheek-to-cheek, we paced back and forth, or swayed gently to a weeping guitar, as I cast longing looks up at the ceiling, picturing Lillian soundly asleep in our bed.

I hated getting up. But I got up anyway, accepting the physical hardship as a nasty but necessary part of caring for Annie the only way possible, the way a mother would. *I* was responsible. She was *my* charge, around the clock. I could not breast-feed her, but I could do everything else. Certainly I could serve as porter between the bassinet and the bed, where Lillian preferred to nurse her. And since Lillian was our sole means of support, the breadwinner, paid to be alert and ready to go to work each morning, it was only logical that I drew the graveyard shift at home.

I understood that. I was well aware of the bargain that Lillian and I had made, but that knowledge did not make getting up any easier. In those early-morning hours, trying to get Annie to sleep, I wondered if I hadn't been a little naïve, a little too hasty. Ruefully, I imagined myself a tenderfoot at a dude ranch who, after an exhilarating ride around the corral on Old Swayback, had signed on for a major trail drive to the railhead. Whoa, there, pardner! Who had saddled whom with what here?

On that first Monday of my two years at home with our baby, I felt decidedly ambivalent about the job that lay ahead. I was eager to get on with being a househusband, but at the same time I feared the unknown. There seemed so much I didn't know about infants, about children. And that was only half of my ignorance, the half I was able to appreciate. There was much about *me* I didn't know, either.

I would learn. In my total-immersion course in fatherhood, I would learn about being a mother. As I became familiar with diaper rash and fits of colic and finger food and water play, I would learn to get out of bed like a robot; to cope with my estrangement from men and my difference from women; to conquer my resentment of Lillian's job and her freedom to leave the house each day for the office. In caring for a child, I would see, there is no woman's work or man's work. There is just work, and responsibility, and bad hours, and small rewards that appear like sudden snowflakes and then quickly go glimmering by. But the rewards come repeatedly, and I learned to catch them and examine them closely. There is mystery in a life at home with a baby, and daily revelation, and tedium and routine, and, in diaphanous

Just a Baby, Only a Man

bursts, pure pleasure. At times, love and contentment welled up from within me, unexpectedly filling my eyes. At other times I sat alone and turned inward, inexplicably sad, strangely warm in a womb of self-pity.

Until becoming a father, I had never known such small turnings, such keenly felt ups and downs. Together Annie and I grew into partners, two separate beings finely tuned, invisibly meshed. As a parent, I learned to feel competent and adventurous, and proud and daring. I felt self-assuredly masculine and amazingly maternal. In time I would feel a new reverence for nature and life, and wonder how I had previously failed to notice the awesome power of infants to flourish and persist.

But on that first Monday as a full-time househusband, I just felt tired.

In the kitchen I filled the kettle with water as yellow leaves from the black walnut trees fluttered by the window. The limber tops of the white pines swayed in the breeze. The day would be freshly cool. The fall term at Bexley College was a week old, and, ready or not, a slender, vivacious, thirty-year-old woman, still rocky from the birth of her first child, would resume her desk in a second-floor office of a sand-colored building set on campus between pine trees. Her name and title were on the door: Dr. Lillian Buchanan, Associate Director, Advising, Counseling and Career Development. Her duties were on her mind. A career-exploration workshop was scheduled for Wednesday; students troubled by grades, parents, and romance had been asking about her return; and her secretary had reported that the computer center had finally run the results of the alumni occupational survey. A stack of printouts was on her desk.

Two weeks of maternity leave were all that she thought she could afford. If she could not finish her work in eight hours, or found herself too tired at first to put in a full day, she would bring work home. I was used to seeing computer cards on the dining-room table, students in the living room, Lillian on the telephone. She liked her work, and felt comfortable when it surrounded her. She did not stint.

I saw work differently. As a journalist, I loved to write, but I was wary of long-term entanglements. The measure of transience granted newspaper reporters suited me. Showing up at the same office at the same time, five days a week, and plying a trade for a wage was a regimen I figured should be engaged in periodically, set off by intervals of semiemployment, called free-lancing, and changes of location.

In the five years since Lillian and I had met in San Francisco—where she was a rehabilitation counselor for the state, and I sold an occasional magazine article to live on the ragged fringe of subsistence—we had alternated the task of making our living. When she worked at counseling, I could write about the family of gorillas at the zoo, or spend the day in a darkroom developing pictures. When I worked for a newspaper, she could be a full-time student.

We had moved to Michigan on Lillian's turn to work. As she began her job in a town of 10,000 people, I began a journalism fellowship at the University of Michigan in Ann Arbor, one hundred and twenty miles away. The program, sponsored by the National Endowment for the Humanities, allowed experienced journalists to drop out of the news business and into academia, where for a year they could luxuriate in the arts, literature, and philosophy while reassessing their careers. I won the fellowship, in part, on the strength of my proposal to study the work ethic. I was fascinated with the nature of work, its appeal, and what made some jobs satisfying and others drudgery. Although I seemed to enjoy my work as a reporter, I wasn't sure why.

When, as we had planned, Lillian became pregnant soon after the year began, I secretly began to violate the spirit of

Just a Baby, Only a Man

the fellowship. I continued my studies of history and sociology and philosophy, but I also knew that I was no longer recharging my batteries for a quick return to my newspaper career. I began to consider a whole new career altogether. During discussions in sociology class on workers' need for a sense of achievement, I began to wonder about the difficulty of tending a baby. While listening to a lunchtime lecture on the changing shape of the family, I contemplated my future role as a father. On the two-hour drive back home each weekend, I thought about my new job. Should I describe myself as a househusband, or would just "father" do?

That I would stay home with our baby seemed never in doubt. Lillian had a job; she could not handle the work of a baby, too. I was available. But could a *man* handle the work of childcare? Could *I*? Was childcare really work? Did it even offer the makings of a career? From my studies in Ann Arbor, I knew what the social researchers said made a job satisfying: autonomy, status, opportunity for advancement, mental challenge, social atmosphere, having one's work valued. Could life at home with a baby offer any of that? Measured against those criteria, housespousing not only sounded like a bad job, it sounded like a bad joke.

But I still wanted the position. The duties, the responsibilities, the isolation, the hours, the routine, the anonymity —they would be the same for me as they were for millions of women. But there was a difference: I was a man. To my mind, gender alone lent my staying home a titillating air of rebelliousness and intrigue. I would have an adventure. Back in the meditative surroundings of the university, sharing pints of beer with other students in the rathskeller, I waxed confident that I could mine nuggets of satisfaction and reward where others had found only noise, clutter, and frustration. I would be able to do this not only because I was a man, a novelty in the role, but because I was a volunteer.

DADDY'S HOME

Months later, standing in the kitchen, rumpled, grumpy, my eyes scratchy, I was about to put my academic theory to the test.

The burner on the stove glowed red. Droplets of water on the kettle hissed as they fell onto the rings and disappeared. Seeping in under the window over the sink, a breeze from the northwest touched my face with an invigorating hint of the cold that would soon seal us indoors in sweaters and storm windows.

I spotted a pair of blackburnian warblers flitting through the yellowing leaves of the walnut tree by the back porch and, while watching them, became aware of Christine Butler next door. She was in her robe, in the kitchen of a college-owned house that was a mirror of our own. Her two boys, aged five and two, sat at the table on either side of a gallon jug of milk. Christine seemed to be scraping Cheerios back into the box, a stern expression on her face.

Today, I thought, I would begin to learn what Christine Butler knew. I would begin to tap into the arcane wisdom of motherhood, to explore the particular realm of women and home and babies, a world of which men knew so little. What an intrepid explorer I was; what an innocent man!

When Annie finished her breakfast, Lillian hollered that she was headed for the shower. I went upstairs and changed Annie's diaper and oiled the stump of her umbilical cord. It was about ready to drop off.

In a pink lounge suit that emphasized the redness of her face, Annie looked particularly feisty and rambunctious. I carried her down to the kitchen, and, from a plastic seat on the counter, she watched me drop two slices of toast into the toaster.

"We're on our own today, kid," I said. "How do you feel?"

Just a Baby, Only a Man

She worked her arms and legs, humming like a little engine. Her eyes wandered around my face. I mugged for her.

Although sure there were adventures to come over the next two years, I did not expect much initial excitement. Except for Lillian's absence, I expected the day to be routine, like the twelve that had preceded it. Annie would sleep most of the time. When awake, she would nurse or take water from me, exercise, gurgle and spit, appear to smile, and begin fussing over unseen discomforts.

The prospects were for more menial drudgery than high adventure. I would be called on to hold and rock her, walk her around the house, change her diaper, and anoint the diaper rash that had popped out on the insides of her thighs. I would be responsible for her, *en garde* against a sudden fit of choking, or the outbreak of fever. But I did not anticipate any emergency.

When Annie did not need me, I could figure out something to have for lunch and dinner, put a load of clothes in the washing machine, make the bed, wash last night's dishes, and vacuum the carpet. The still-laden tomato plants by the house needed watering, and the fern in the living room could have used a trim.

I would read and write. We had collected a shelf-ful of how-to-parent books, and already the reflections of fatherhood were backing up in my mind. I planned to concentrate first on recording my impressions of infancy in Annie's scrapbook and on writing letters to family and friends. In a few days, I thought, I would call a Sunday magazine editor in Detroit and toss out some story ideas.

Lillian walked into the dining room as I slid a plate of toast onto the table.

"Hey, you look great," I said.

"This skirt feels funny. It doesn't seem to fit right."

"You show a little postpartum droop, perhaps. But you look fine."

In a dark blue jacket and skirt and white-collared blouse, she looked crisply professional. Only the drawn look deep in her green-flecked eyes marred the picture of the consummate career woman, off to the marketplace.

"What about me?" I wondered aloud.

Lillian appraised me with a flourish. I was wearing a red, paint-streaked T-shirt, wrinkled from sleep, and a pair of jeans patched on one knee with a yellow insignia from a manufacturer of earthmoving equipment. My feet were bare, my hair disheveled.

"You look—comfortable, natural, appropriate," she said. "You look fine, too."

The contrast between us appealed to me, underscoring the juxtaposition of our roles. I *was* off on an adventure.

"You want some cereal?"

"No, I'd better get going."

"Have some toast, anyway."

She took a gulp of the coffee. "I'll take the toast with me. Where's Annie?"

"Oh," I said, remembering her with a start. She was still sitting on the counter in the kitchen, amusing herself. We walked Lillian to the door.

"Call Jim sometime today and ask when he wants to see us, okay?"

"Right," I said.

Lillian picked up her briefcase from the steps and leaned in to give us each a kiss. "I'll see you about ten-thirty for a feeding."

Annie and I stood at the living room window and watched her walk across the street to the campus. She turned twice to wave. When she finally disappeared behind a shimmering screen of maples by the Administration Building, I felt a sudden urge to run outside, to cut loose with a surge of energy, to run. Outside, I thought, I could shuck the veil of fatigue and suck in the cool air that would sharpen my senses and tune me for the day. If something *was* going to happen on my first day on the job alone, I wanted to be ready.

On the way to the kitchen, where I planned to point out the warblers to Annie, I kicked open the newspaper that Lillian had pitched aside. Monday, a notoriously slow news day. The lead story suggested that an aide to President Carter had used bank-owned airplanes to travel to football games. The International Monetary Fund had issued a statement on lending rates and unemployment. Ethiopia reported heavy fighting in the desert. That was about it. Nothing.

I could imagine reporters and editors in newsrooms everywhere, praying for action. Reporters were working the phones, prodding sources, pleading for a break. Editors turned ghoulish.

"We need something live, a good plane crash or something," an assistant city desk chief was saying somewhere. "Who's got an ax murder for me?"

Those were the days when I would be ordered to make a phone survey of gasoline prices, or crank out ten inches on the upper-atmosphere weather pattern. I was glad not to be there.

From the kitchen window, I scanned the walnut tree, but the warblers were gone. "You couldn't see them anyway," I told Annie. "I don't think you can see that far."

The warblers made me think of music; that seemed an appropriate way to start the day. I put Annie down in a wooden cradle in the living room and picked out an Eric Clapton record. When the needle dropped, I sank into the armchair beside her and nudged the cradle into a gentle sway. Soaring runs of clear, clean guitar ran around the living room, pulling me into a slide-show reverie. I found myself recalling a tough, long-haired pub band in Australia, and then a windy stretch of white sand dunes on a beach. I remembered flying alone around the world after leaving a newsroom in Perth, and a hot refueling stop in Bahrain where a planeload of Russian tourists were buying postcards from a man in a burnoose. I recalled a half-cocked plan for a Caribbean idyll that fell apart on a Florida beach, leaving me near-broke and hurt and sure that I could do without any help from anyone. Those days of solitary romanticism seemed so empty now, so far away, so long before I had a child.

When I became aware of the silence, Annie was asleep. I covered her with a knit blanket and bounded up the stairs to the typewriter in the study. Needing to talk, I talked in letters.

How am I doing so far? Lil has been gone for an hour, and I am yet to call for help, the police, or quits. We are clockwork. Annie sleeps and I write, just as planned. And you thought I might be in over my head just because I didn't know any babies personally. What is there to know? I may be only a man, but she is just a baby.

The books warn me: The first several years of life are pivotal, but the first two critical. This, in other words, is where I can screw up irrevocably and never know it until Annie, at thirteen, announces her ambition is to be a Dallas Cowboys cheerleader. Aaaaagh. Where did I go wrong? That diaper pin in her thigh, or should I have spent more time reading to her from *The Life of Emma Goldman,* anarchist?

I'm in a B-grade jungle movie. My line: "Sure is quiet out there tonight." "Yeah, too quiet," says someone else. But what happens next? I dunno. And Annie? What does she know?

What Annie knew was in her genes, her blood, her heart. She weighed a little more than eight pounds, and although she was a certified live birth, a census statistic, she was really

Just a Baby, Only a Man

less a person than a helpless body of unwired neurons and unintegrated circuits. The parts were all there, but everything was not hooked up yet. She was filled with instincts, but not intelligence. Without thinking, she knew where to find her mother's milk. She would grasp an object placed in her hand, and when held upright she would move her legs as if walking. She involuntarily startled each time I accidentally kicked the diaper pail beside her crib. She could not hold her head up. The continents of her skull had not yet come together to seal the topmost fontanel.

Although Annie might have some sense of Lillian or me, by smell or the feel of our hands, she could not pick either one of us out of a lineup. She may have thought we were one all-provident being, sometimes the gentle source of warm milk, and at other times a darker visage who spoke in a rumble. She knew nothing of men or women, mothers and fathers, or the roles each traditionally played. She was not aware of the expectations that accompanied the birth of boys and girls. She did not know she was now a child of unorthodoxy.

I would write a few lines, then stop. During the stops, the quiet made me uneasy and I would run downstairs to check on Annie. Each time I got up, Katydog followed, sensing that something was about to happen that she did not want to miss. And each time, disappointed, she followed me back upstairs, sat, and stared at me, her head cocked inquisitively. Finally she unnerved me so that I banished her to the end of a chain outside the house.

At 10:30, Lillian walked in the front door and shouted, "Hello!" Annie took her cue and began to cry.

"How did it go?" Lillian removed her jacket and sat down with Annie on the couch. She unbuttoned her blouse, opened the flap of her brassiere, and Annie's yowl subsided into a contented slurp.

"Nothing happened. She slept, and I wrote part of a letter."
"Good. Did you call Jim?"
"No, damn, I forgot. I will."
"I can do it from the office."
"No, no. I'll do it. I had time. I just forgot."
"Well, I started in on an evaluation report, and made two counseling appointments for this afternoon."
"You're going to be busier than I am," I said. I almost felt I should apologize for not doing my share.
"Don't look for a part-time job yet. It's like being on standby. You may not get to fly, but you have to be there."

My next thirty days as a househusband went skipping along like the first. When Annie wasn't sleeping, or snuggled to Lillian's breast, I was rocking her, or looking at her, or showing her pictures, or putting rattles in her hand, or changing her diaper. Much of the time when she was awake, I was doing something designed to get her back to sleep again.

When she did sleep, I cooked, washed clothes and dishes, picked up books and shoes and receiving blankets, raked leaves outside, or went to the basement darkroom to print pictures of Annie, often just hours after I had taken them.

There was, in those early days, a lot of time. I often found myself sunk deep in an easy chair, ignoring a book in my hands, dreamily wondering what might be coming up that night on television, or thinking of someone we should invite over for dinner. The quick confidence I gained in my ability to handle the chores of househusbandry pleased me. My suppositions about the job were reinforced by experience. Caring for an infant was work that a man could handle. It was not difficult. It did not require years of training or experience, or being female. There were no heart-stopping emergencies. In fact, on most days, nothing very much happened at all. And *that* began to concern me. Would raising a child turn out to be a bore?

Finally, in Annie's sixth week, when something did happen, it made me furious. Twenty-six bright red, smooth pimples broke out on the summit of her cheeks, thirteen on each. They represented the first serious challenge to my competence as a father. I took it hard.

"Lil!"

Annie lay on her back in a stream of morning sunlight that streaked across our bed. "Good God, come look at this!"

Responding to the alarm in my voice, Lillian ran in from the bathroom expecting calamity. "What?" she cried.

"This," I said with disgust, pointing to the blight. "Some creeping crud, or something. The kid's got acne."

Lillian sighed with relief. "I couldn't imagine—I was preparing myself for blood, or something serious."

"Look at this. It *is* serious."

"It's a rash. Look it up in Spock. It's probably nothing."

I flipped through our Bible, *Baby and Child Care,* hungry for salvation. Under "Mild face rashes," I found an inch of deliverance.

> Then there are collections of a few small red spots or smooth pimples on the cheeks. These may last a long time and get a parent quite upset. At times they fade and then get red again. Different ointments don't seem to do much good, but these spots always go away eventually.

"That's all it says. Six hundred sixty-six pages in this book, and this—this *fungus* gets part of a paragraph. It's hard to get Spock excited, isn't it?"

"It's nothing," said Lillian. "Only worth a couple of lines."

DADDY'S HOME

"But it looks so ugly."

"It's obviously not bothering Annie. And it's not your fault."

"Yeah, but who's going to know that?"

Those "few red spots or smooth pimples on the cheeks" were the worst case of dermatitis *I* had ever experienced. I realized just how much they bothered me two days later when I bundled Annie up in a snowsuit and took her out for a walk. The temperature was barely above forty degrees, but the sky was clear and I thought the sun would help.

Neighbor Christine and Nat, her five-year-old, intercepted us as we made a pass by the house in the stroller.

"Look at this big girl, Nat," Christine said admiringly. And to me: "She is growing, isn't she?"

"Gained more than a pound already," I said proudly.

"I would take that as a compliment."

"Thank you, I will."

Christine bent over for a closer look. Annie's face was a ruddy oval surrounded by a green knit cap tied under her chin. Except for those pimples, she looked impeccable. Impulsively, I decided to launch a preemptive confession.

"She has a rash," I said. Trying to sound casual, I wanted to preclude any chance that Christine might suspect there was something about Annie's condition that I was not aware of or attending to.

"I see."

What did she mean by that? I wondered. Was there a note of accusatory concern in her voice, or was I becoming paranoid?

"Staphylococcus," I said, matter-of-factly. "Jim says it's very common. And Spock says there is nothing to do. It'll disappear."

"I know, but it's worrisome," she said.

"What's the matter with her?" asked Nat.

Just a Baby, Only a Man

"Nothing, darling," said Christine quickly. "She just has a rash."

Afraid of sounding too defensive, I suppressed an urge to say more. Christine knew, as I knew, that outbreaks like this were common in infancy. They were transitory, had no lasting consequences. So why did I take it so personally?

"Say, I see you were up late last night."

"Yeah. I hope the music wasn't too loud," I said.

"No, our bedrooms are on the other side of the house. I was just up getting a drink for one of the kids when I saw your light."

"Colic," I said, shaking my head. "Miserable."

Colic had just sprung up as my other cross. It made us all miserable, but I figured no one, not even Annie, was more miserable with it than I. Apparently content one minute, without warning she would unleash a torrent of gut-wrenching cries so excruciating that immediately I wanted to join her in sympathy and self-pity. She often cried for an hour without pause.

If colic struck late in the evening, after we had all gone to bed, I got up. I searched my heart for charity while walking the little banshee up and down the living room.

Music, played loudly, almost always helped quiet her, as long as we kept moving. We danced to Van Morrison, Jeff Beck, and the Rolling Stones. I thought the rock 'n' roll heartbeat reminded her of the womb, comforted her, somehow soothed the pains of a body still struggling to find its own rhythm. Little Feat sang: *"There's a fat man in the bathtub with the bluuu-ze,"* and I imagined a leviathan in the shape of a naked Orson Welles sinking deeply into hot water, seeking respite from the sounds of a tortured child who would not be consoled.

In frustration, I turned again to Dr. Spock, and again he gave me succor.

> Parents are distressed to have their babies so unhappy and think something is terribly wrong. They wonder how long a child can keep this up and not become exhausted. They wonder how long *they* can stand it. . . .
> The most important thing is for the mother and father to recognize that the condition is fairly common, that it doesn't seem to do the baby any permanent harm, that, on the contrary, it occurs most often in babies that are developing and growing well, and that it will probably be gone before the baby is three months old, if not before. . . .

Before long, I had read that section on colic so often that I knew much of it by heart. I especially liked the line "They wonder how long *they* can stand it," and during many a late-night dance I would repeat it softly to Annie, trying to calm her and myself with the balm of authority.

"Except for colic and that stubborn rash, we're doing fine," I told Christine.

"They'll pass," she said knowingly. "All the kids go through it, and somehow they survive. Wait till you get to chicken pox and the measles."

"Sounds like fun."

"You do seem to have adopted the maternal attitude, though. You're worrying a lot."

"No, not really," I lied, wanting to draw a line between responsible concern and obsession.

"It's all right. It's natural," she said with firm reassurance. "It's what mothers do. They worry, as if worrying were what kept real tragedy from striking. Only after the rash and the colic pass do you realize how silly it all seemed."

"You're a real philosopher, Christine."

"No, just a mother. Like you."

Chapter 2

The Domestic Pioneer

CHRISTINE BUTLER always seemed to me an unlikely housewife. She was an eastern boarding school girl, a Vassar graduate with a master's degree in art. She wore her brown hair to her waist, disliked shoes, and was determinedly insouciant.

I figured she should have been something of a feminist. But she wasn't. At twenty-eight, she had two sons and a preoccupied husband who taught college psychology, and if there had ever been a time when she'd thought playing second fiddle to her spouse was anything but a noble life, the time was long past. She had made a deal to hold up her end of a traditional marriage, and she stuck to it. She met Dick's expressions of displeasure over a messy house or a late dinner with equanimity. She was unflaggingly cheerful.

From the window of our study, I often saw Christine standing over the sink or sweeping up crumbs from the dining-room floor or, sometimes—when the boys were in bed—drawing in ink at the kitchen table. Although I did not feel spiritually close to her (I found her subservience to Dick unsettling), I liked Christine. Despite our differences in realpolitik, she seemed to accept without hesitation my role as housespouse. As a wife and mother, she was a model of competence, and offered advice without being didactic. I felt better knowing she was next door.

One day in her kitchen, when Annie was napping and I had run over to borrow a crepe pan, she told me that Dick thought Lillian and I were the most fascinating couple he knew.

"Really?"

"Yes. He thinks it's neat the way you've switched roles."

"We don't think we ever had any set roles to switch," I said, making the fine point, "since we never were in a traditional setup. But we have reversed tradition."

"That's what Dick thinks is so interesting. I'm like you: I don't think it makes any difference who takes care of the children or who works, as long as each person is happy. But Dick does."

Dick would have made a splendid Victorian patriarch, I sneered to myself.

"Who does he think is in danger, me or Annie?" I smiled.

Christine laughed. "I don't know if he sees any danger. He's just curious. You know, he's a researcher. Everything is potential evidence."

"Evidence of what?" A spot of annoyance began to spread across the front of my mind.

"I don't know," said Christine, now wishing she had let

The Domestic Pioneer

the subject lie. "He's probably just interested to see how a man does in a woman's job, that's all."

"Woman's job?"

"What is *usually* a woman's job."

"Oh, I see," I said, surprising myself with the sharpness of my tone.

Christine looked away, thoroughly uncomfortable. Now I felt guilty. Why pick on her when it was her husband who bothered me?

"Well, anything for science," I said, heading for the door.

"What kind of crepes are you going to make?" Christine asked cheerfully.

"I'm not sure. I have some frozen peaches. I just saw a recipe in a magazine I thought I might try."

"Crepes aren't hard," she said.

"Good. Thanks for the pan."

Back in my own kitchen, I twirled Christine's pan down the countertop and knew that the crepe-making mood had been overcome by events. I retreated to the study to await Annie's call.

I thought about Dick. He was a big, shambling fellow who cut his own hair, wore tweed jackets through the summer, and, whenever I talked to him, seemed to be trying to recall something he had forgotten to do. He was three years younger than I, but looked and acted much older, I was sure.

In a small department, kept small by its elitist chairman, Dick Butler was known as an exception. He not only had a reputation as a good teacher, but he cared about students and made time for them—more time, it seemed, than he made for his family. He spent many evenings with his students in the basement of the science building supervising experiments on rats after tinkering with their brains.

Dick was an observer, clinically detached. When our friends Roger and Susan Vander kidded us about being their guinea pigs, I knew they were genuinely interested in our arrangement for work and childcare. But I had the impression that Dick saw us as a serendipitous case study. While Roger and Susan wanted our setup to work, and give them an option, Dick looked at us with professional disinterest. His hypothesis might have predicted some malfunctioning of our family that would lend credence to his theory that sex roles were not interchangeable.

To Dick, we may have had pink eyes and numbered tags on our ears.

I stared at the portable Royal typewriter in front of me and recalled the woman who had given it to me years earlier in San Francisco. She was standing on the sidewalk surrounded by two large suitcases, several cardboard boxes, and a six-foot floor lamp.

"Hey, are you a writer?" she had shouted at me from across Post Street as I ambled downhill.

"Me?"

"Yeah. If you're a writer, do you want a typewriter?" She held up a square black case.

She was dressed like a secretary, in a skirt and pullover top. She was about twenty-five. She did not look like a street crazy. But living a marginal existence as a free-lancer, just managing each week to come up with my $39 room rent, I had learned to be suspicious of everyone. I did not want to be drawn into some con.

"What's the matter with it?"

"Nothing, for God's sake! I just got evicted, and I can't haul all this shit around. You want it or not?"

Back in my room, I was amazed to find the typewriter worked perfectly. More amazing to me, however, was that she had known I was a writer. How had she known that? Did my beard signal "writer"? Was it the long, scraggly hair, or the knit cap, or the denim, or the orange knapsack I carried, full of papers and paperbacks and story ideas?

I never knew. I still don't know. I looked very much like a thousand other men wandering up and down San Francisco's hills in 1970. Perhaps there was a reflective air about me, or in my eyes the inquiring gleam of the chronicler.

Perhaps she just wanted to get rid of a typewriter.

In any case, the incident reaffirmed my calling; I used the gift of the typewriter as evidence for what I did, just as Dick used evidence to test his hypotheses. Journalism was a trade that not only provided me with a livelihood but also provided a rationale for almost anything I did: I was a writer, always collecting material.

Suddenly I felt I had been too hard on Dick. He was probably no more curious about us than anyone else who thought my role as housespouse was out of the ordinary. Perhaps he found us amusing. Perhaps he just saw us as the weirdos next door.

Even as a full-time father, I was a journalist. Since before Annie's birth, my reporting about her had been limited to letters, most of them long, rambling discourses on the wonders of parenthood and Annie's progress through the journey up the subtle grade of infancy. I made copies of my dispatches and, with up-to-the-week photographs, sent them to Lillian's parents, who farm an orange grove in central California, and to my parents, who lived a suburban life outside Akron, Ohio. Duplicates went to Lillian's sister, my brother and sister, other relatives and friends. What I soon had going was a chain letter, and on behalf of each recipient I assumed an interest in Annie only slightly less than my own.

Once named to my mailing list, there was no getting off. The letters flew with such frequency that some recipients must have wondered if I had anything else to do. But writing letters was my daily constitutional, the means by which I not only documented Annie and how she grew but also tried to understand my own feelings about being a father. I ran to the typewriter to unburden myself, to make sense of what I had just seen or realized or felt. Sometimes when I sat down at the Royal, I went to confession, and other times I went to analysis. Either way, I needed to go.

Annie was down on the floor in the middle of a blue blanket this morning, and I sat down on the couch and watched her like an Amazonian Indian might watch television, like magic. She looked like a beached sea turtle, working her arms and legs as if flapping for the surf. I could imagine Marlin Perkins in a classroom: "Notice the extension of the legs here," lightly touching the back of her knees with a pointer, "and see how her back arches as she lifts her head off the floor. Fascinating."
Sometimes I can almost fancy myself a visiting anthropologist, studying Annie as if she were a subject I could dispassionately write about. But then I find myself near to tears with love for her; whatever I said about her would be rejected as hopelessly contaminated with love.
There seems to be no sign that Lillian's absence, or my care, have led to any social or physical retardation. She smiles now; it's not gas. She likes me! Who said a man couldn't handle this job?

Who, besides me and Lillian, said a man *could* handle this job?
In the books on childcare, men were barely mentioned. Househusbands, and even fathers, were tossed in as footnotes or incidentally dealt with somewhere in the back, between the section on "Special Problems" and the index. At most, fathers were bit players who periodically walked on stage to chuck baby on the chin and coax out a smile. When the kids were older, fathers could roughhouse a little. But they did not keep house, and they certainly did not take care of the children.

The Domestic Pioneer

"The father knows even less than his wife," the authors of *The First Twelve Months of Life* declared with dismissive certainty.

Although there was no evidence that fathers were capable of doing what I did, some experts *supposed* that men could handle childcare. Except for breast-feeding, a man can fill the woman's role, said Burton L. White in *The First Three Years of Life*, "because when you look closely at what it means to be a child-rearer in the child's first three years, you find that most of the factors involved do not seem to be sex-linked. Designing a home that is safe and interesting for a child does not require male or female genes."

Spock was of the same opinion. Referring to home- and childcare, he wrote: "There is no reason why fathers shouldn't be able to do these jobs as well as mothers, and contribute equally to the children's security and development."

It seemed so obvious. Of course, a man could rear children. Of course, there was nothing in running a safe and interesting home that required male or female genes. How elementary! How commonsensical! I was doing it!

But why was there no proof? Why were the experts just supposing? Either there had never been enough men involved in childcare to make up a large enough sample to study, or the phenomenon was not deemed worthy of study.

Perhaps the scientific community was waiting for Dick to break the news, and the news was us.

Surveying our collection of books on children and parents, I found one sole smidgen of evidence that a man could mother a child. Unfortunately, the evidence came not from a study of humans but from rhesus monkeys. To back up their contention that "the newborn has no innate preference for one parent or another," the authors of *Father Power* cite an experiment in which monkeys took food from an ersatz mother made of wire, but, once satiated, left the source of nourishment to snuggle up to a dummy mother of terry cloth.

That was the proof I could succeed as a househusband; I did not need lactating breasts. If I needed any more solid support than that, I thought, I could be in trouble.

Feeling like the Ancient Mariner—"Alone, alone, all, all alone/Alone on a wide, wide sea!"—I went downstairs and began to cut up a chicken for tetrazzini. Cutting away fat and stripping the skin, I wondered if I was at that hour the only man in America standing in his kitchen preparing dinner while his child napped and his wife was at work. Surely there were others—hundreds, maybe thousands. But we all stood alone.

Lillian rushed through the front door, her right arm pressed across her chest. "Where is that girl?" she demanded.

I thought for an instant she had been injured. "What happened?"

"I am leaking like crazy. Soaked my blouse. Where is she?"

"Upstairs."

"Please bring her down. This is painful."

I ran upstairs and grabbed Annie from her crib. Her eyes fluttered and she began smacking her lips as we descended. "Food," I said when her eyes opened. "Chow time."

"Ah," sighed Lillian when Annie began to relieve the pressure. "I thought I was going to die. Four o'clock, comes the flood. We've got to get a breast pump."

"Where were you?"

"In the middle of a staff meeting. I could feel my bra getting wet, and then the blouse, and finally I just got up, excused myself, and ran. Rod made some smirking remark about wishing he could help."

The Domestic Pioneer

Rod, a counselor in Lillian's office, was an enthusiastic womanizer who assumed that sex was never any further from the minds of others than it was from his.

"What are you making?"

"Tetrazzini. I was thinking about trying some crepes for dessert, but Dick destroyed my culinary ambitions."

"Dick? What was he doing here?"

"He wasn't here. I was talking to Christine and she mentioned that Dick found us fascinating. He thinks of us as some kind of experimental research grouping."

"I'm glad we're useful."

"Yeah, that's what I thought." I sat down in a chair opposite Lillian. "But, you know, there isn't any research on the subject."

"Of men caring for children? Having doubts? That doesn't sound like you."

"I'm just curious," I said, not adding that I was also interested to find out just how rare I was.

"There are the Trobriand Islanders. Men there do childcare."

"They do? Maybe we can form a co-op."

"It's in the South Pacific. But look in Margaret Mead. It's upstairs in the bookcase under the window."

Lillian changed her blouse and returned to the office, and Annie and I trudged upstairs. I propped her in a corner of the study so that she could sit and watch me, and I pulled out Mead's *Male and Female*.

"Hey, kiddo, listen to this," I said, my finger on an underlined passage from the chapter called "Human Fatherhood Is a Social Invention": " 'Somewhere at the dawn of human history, some social invention was made under which males started nurturing females . . . and their young.'

"That's what I'm doing."

Annie made a staccato clucking sound and blinked her

eyes at the light on the desk. She seemed to be ignoring me. I took a dumbbell-shaped rattle from my shirt pocket and put it in her hand. She immediately put one end in her mouth.

I flipped through the book, scanning Lillian's underlinings. In "To Both Their Own," I found Mead warning that a man reckless enough to engage in women's work would be diminished in the eyes of others and was likely to end up doubting his manhood. And as if that were not discouragement enough, she went on to suggest that for a man practicing a feminine occupation, "the whole symbolic system, within which the novice must work, facilitates every step taken by the expected sex, obstructs every step taken by the unexpected sex."

"My God, Annie, that's me! I'm the 'unexpected sex'! It sounds like a mutation."

Annie looked at me blankly, unconcerned. As she tried to swallow the rattle, the bulbous end made her cheeks puff out like a chipmunk at harvest time. If she wasn't worried, why should I be? Just because some South Sea Islanders led Margaret Mead to believe that a man who took on women's work would be thought a fool, would surrender his self-respect, and make a mess of the job anyway? No. "What, me worry?" I thought, like *Mad* magazine's Alfred E. Neuman.

"We'd better go back downstairs and concentrate on dinner," I said, picking her up. "Let's see if I can finish up this tetrazzini without screwing up."

When Lillian returned, I told her that Mead had been no help. "She says I'm going to fail. She says I'll probably have to have my ego rebuilt. To say nothing of what might happen to Annie."

"Well, it's an old book," said Lillian. "But somewhere there are accounts of the Trobriand Island men taking care

The Domestic Pioneer

of children, and they remain very masculine and their family life is very stable."

"Very comforting," I said, loudly dramatic. "Who needs 'em, anyway? I'll go it alone, fearless, stouthearted, just me and my baby, the Little Nipper and the Domestic Pioneer." I set my jaw and struck a haughty pose.

"You're a rock," teased Lillian as she shifted Annie to her shoulder and headed upstairs to change clothes. "A brick."

Dinner would be late. I put the chicken in the pressure cooker, turned the burner on high, and stared out the window while absently rinsing mushrooms.

Who was I really? What would I say if asked to describe myself? Could I write a capsule biography for the Who's Who of Homebodies? Who was this Domestic Pioneer?

The Domestic Pioneer was the bearded, wild-haired man I often saw in the mirror when straightening up from the toilet bowl, Annie in one hand and a wrung-out diaper in the other.

He was the former football player and hurdler with scar tissue over one eye and two knees full of cinders, who had learned to hold his daughter like an extension of himself, to soothe her by coaxing out a satisfying burp, or to rock away her fretfulness, or to tickle her neck with his moustache and make her giggle.

He was the yeoman who kept house; who picked up and swept up and scraped up; who hauled the trash to the curb on Monday and the dirty diapers to the front porch on Wednesday; who laundered his daughter's sleepers and his wife's blouses; who made mushroom quiche for dinner and cornbread for lunch; who clipped coupons for the supermarket's weekly specials; who deposited his wife's paycheck and paid the bills on time.

The Domestic Pioneer was a househusband without a community of male peers, or a sense of his occupational

DADDY'S HOME

history. He did not know exactly how he was doing as a full-time father.

The Domestic Pioneer was the man who occasionally feared he was not being taken seriously. He was the same man who had volunteered to organize refreshments for the Lamaze Class reunion so he would get the attention he deserved.

And then he called his wife at work to get her approval.

"You?" said Lillian. "Refreshments?"

"My kingdom takes in all things domestic," I explained. "Refreshments are my business."

"Well, good," she said, with almost the right amount of enthusiasm. "Sounds like you."

I had telephoned the home of each of the couples in our class, talked to nine mothers, and suggested that each bring her specialty, be it cookies, cake, bread, or similar teatime food. To one woman who said she did not have time to bake, I assigned punch. Another said she would bring a punch bowl and cups.

The arrangements were handled expeditiously and assertively, I thought. Everyone was involved, and everyone planned to attend. There would be plenty of people and plenty of food. I would bake three loaves of banana nut bread myself.

At 2:00 P.M. on Sunday, under a metallic late-fall sky, we drove five miles out of town to the flat river-bottom land where Jack and Marge Olson lived. Jack farmed part-time and worked as a machinist, while Marge cared for three children, including their four-week-old boy, born two days after Annie.

Their two-story gabled house, freshly painted, stood out from the brown fields of corn stubble like a castle. Half a dozen cars were already parked in the yard.

As soon as we stepped in the door, I realized that I had

The Domestic Pioneer

made a serious miscalculation. The table in the hallway fairly sagged under the weight of baked goods. Chocolate chip cookies, coffee cake, apple tarts, peanut clusters, even Rice Krispies and marshmallow squares—the scene seemed set for a downtown bake sale.

"Mike, what is the plan with the food here?" Marge indicated the bounty, much of it still in cookie tins or wrapped in foil. I held Annie in the crook of my arm. Beside me, Lillian stood with a brown paper bag containing the three loaves of bread.

"I haven't seen this much food in one house since our family Fourth of July picnic was rained out two years ago," said Marge. "But we had a hundred and ten people here for that."

"Well," I said, hoping to joke my way through the embarrassment, "we can all have a dessert exchange with the leftovers."

"Did you ask *everyone* to bake something?" She looked incredulous.

"No, no, not everyone." I pulled a crumpled list from my pocket. "Jane is bringing a drink, and Emily is bringing cups."

"I'll just put this bread right here," said Lillian, barely containing her amusement. "How many loaves do you want to slice for a start?"

By the time all the guests arrived, my inadequacies as director of catering had been forgotten in a maelstrom of children and parents that spun through a deep layering of exclamation and noise. There seemed to be babies everywhere: in arms, on the floor, propped up in corners, and lolling in carrying seats.

Lillian took off Annie's red jacket, revealing a snug, hand-knit suit that made her look bottom-heavy. She seemed drowsy and unalert as I leaned her against a pillow on the floor and sat down beside her. Her naptime was approaching.

Frank Cooper, an affable lawyer who gesticulated grandly with long, slender fingers, was describing the blissful birth of his son, Kevin.

"We hardly even had to get into the heavy-breathing exercises. It was over that fast. Sherrie had no anesthetic, no drugs of any kind. It was a breeze, really." He looked smugly satisfied, as if an easy birth were merely a matter of intelligence.

"That's wonderful," said Joyce McEwan, who had taught us the Lamaze technique of husband-coached childbirth like religion. "But you probably used the exercises and didn't realize it."

"We did some exercises, sure," allowed Frank. "I'm glad we had them. But it never got painful."

"I wonder what Sherrie would say about that," said Marge.

"Hey, really, ask her." Frank called to Sherrie, who came over holding a still bundle in a blue cotton blanket.

"Sherrie, they don't believe me. The birth was no trouble, was it?"

"It went real well," agreed Sherrie. Instead of elaboration, she offered a wan smile.

"Some births are easy," said Joyce. "But you can't count on it."

"My first two, I just had them knock me out," said Marge. "That's why I took the class this time—so I could see what happens."

Joyce turned to me. "What about Annie there? Did she give you much trouble?"

"She was very stubborn," I said. "Twenty-four hours of labor." The group oohed in sympathetic chorus.

"She's still giving us trouble. Now it's colic."

The Domestic Pioneer

"Here," said Sherrie, handing her son to his father. "He's waking up, and I want to get that bottle out of the car."

Frank took his son proudly. "This guy is a champ. He's always peaceful, blissed out like a Buddha. I don't even hear him cry that much at night. When he starts hollering, Sherrie takes him in the next bedroom and gets him quieted down right away."

"You mean you don't get up with him?" I asked in mock surprise.

"Oh, sure I get up sometimes. But I have to go to work in the morning, too. Not like *some* people." He raised an eyebrow at me. "Anyway, what can I do for him? The guy wants a nipple."

Frank leaned back on the couch, cuddling his son. I remembered how his easy humor and his ability to draw laughs had served to make the ten weeks of classes progressively more enjoyable, and even unite a group diverse in education and occupation.

Suddenly, his Buddha erupted in stentorian fury.

"Hey, what's up, kid?" asked Frank, sitting up straight. "Did you eat some of Mike's banana nut bread?"

"He never touched it," I said in defense.

"Hang on, Bozo. Take it easy. She's coming." Frank began to look up from his son's contorted face to the front door.

Joyce slid around beside Frank and began making faces at the baby. Marge seemed to have disappeared.

Annie sat wide-eyed at the commotion, but remained quiet. I found myself smiling.

"You probably scared him, Frank," I said.

"No, he's hungry. Sherrie will be here in a minute."

"Maybe he *ought* to have some banana nut bread. There's plenty."

"Heh-heh," said Frank. He smiled uncomfortably.

DADDY'S HOME

"Uh-oh," said Joyce. "Looks like his diaper is leaking. Watch your jacket there."

"Oh, shit!" said Frank.

"I'll get a towel," said Joyce, heading for the kitchen.

I raised myself off the floor a little to get a better view of the bundle. "Hey, yellowish green. You're breast-feeding, huh?"

"Where in the hell *is* Sherrie?" said Frank, ignoring me. He jiggled the baby like a hot potato.

"Here, take this diaper," I said, pulling one out of the bag beside me.

He tried to wedge the diaper between the baby's bottom and his pale blue jacket. "Damn," he muttered.

"What kind of diaper you got on him, cloth or paper?"

"Hell, I don't know. But it's worthless, whatever it is."

Frank's son cried on with relentless fury. I decided to risk a suggestion.

"Sometimes I get Annie quieted down by changing her position," I said, lifting my voice to be heard. "Up on the shoulder often works."

Frank seemed dazed. He looked at me, but I was not sure he heard.

"Like this," I said, reaching for Annie as my demonstrator. I hoisted my own peaceful child onto my shoulder and gently patted her back.

Frank swung his son's head upright, put a hand on his drooping diaper, and pushed Kevin into the position I had indicated. As the child rose to his shoulder, he trailed a colorful streak the length of Frank's shirtfront that quickly spread onto his jacket. And, if possible, the child's fury increased.

Both father and son now appeared to be in perfect agony. Kevin's painful cries began to draw concerned parents from all over the house. But *my* primary concern lay with Frank;

The Domestic Pioneer

sympathy for his predicament welled within me, and I struggled to come up with another suggestion when Annie suddenly erupted.

Without warning or a warm-up whimper, she began to match Kevin note for breathless note.

"This is great," Frank shouted at me over the din. Anger had replaced exasperation in his eyes.

"He's getting everybody upset," I said, indicating Kevin with undisguised pique. "Here, I know, stand up."

We both struggled to our feet, our children wailing in raucous concert.

"Let's walk," I said. "That usually works."

Frank and I began pacing the living room, stepping over and around legs and plates of cookies and small children, cooing pleas for peace into tiny red ears.

"Hey, Frank, I love the colors in your shirt. Very smart," yelled a male voice.

"You two have a real gift for handling children," laughed someone else.

By the time we had twice run the gauntlet of the living room and I had decided to take Annie outside, something wonderful happened: Both infants grew quiet.

"Hey!" said Frank, his eyes alight. "It worked."

"Yeah," I said, equally thrilled. "Sure it worked."

Sherrie appeared with the diaper bag. "What happened?"

"Kid's leaking poop," said Frank.

"I thought I could hear him crying all the way outside."

"You probably could. But I got him calmed down."

Sherrie took the baby into the bedroom while Frank began mopping up his jacket and shirt with the towel that Joyce had handed him.

"The stuff is odorless," I advised. "It'll wash out."

"*This* is what you do all day?" He shook his head in sympathy and disgust.

DADDY'S HOME

"That's just a part of it. Sometimes it gets *real* messy."

"Next party, I'll know how to dress," he said, looking up with a smile. "And I'll carry an extra diaper."

"Yeah, I learned that lesson in the supermarket one day. Luckily, the paper towels were only an aisle away."

Frank laughed. "Here I am scraping poop off my shirt and getting hints on childcare from a man. Who would have believed it?"

"Who would?" I laughed in return.

On the way out the door, Lillian bagged a selection of chocolate chip cookies and a half-loaf of pumpkin bread.

"Did you enjoy it?" she asked me in the car.

"I did, yes. It was great to see such an array of babies. I talked to Frank for a while."

"How's he doing?"

"Pretty good," I said. "He's got a lot to learn, but he's trying."

Chapter 3

Childcare Mechanics

BY LATE NOVEMBER, the weather had turned nasty—cold and wet. Oak leaves plastered the tennis courts. Gray dawns lingered all day, then deepened to blackness again at 5:30.

Sitting in the afternoon quiet next to Annie's room at naptime, I listened to the furnace kick on and wistfully thought that I would not see another warbler for six months. The long Michigan winter had settled around us like a shroud.

Annie often awoke with her eyes glued shut. She cried angrily at her blindness and I would run in to find her lashes matted and stuck together with a white matter that oozed from her tear ducts. As she screamed in frustration, I used a wet washcloth to break the seal.

Jim Howard, Annie's doctor, said a membrane in the tear ducts had failed to open, causing the discharge that would normally drain through the nose to back up into the eyes. He prescribed a sulfur solution and demonstrated a finger massage. He said the eyes would likely clear.

With that exception, Annie was healthy. Although far below average in weight, she nursed eagerly and regularly. A chart in Jim's office indicated that she was longer than ninety percent of all babies her age. She grew tall and thin, like her parents.

Nearing three months, she could support her head, form most of the vowel sounds, and purposefully strike the wooden beads that hung over her crib. She was resilient, not fragile. Once, when I turned my back on her, she rolled off the ottoman. She was stunned into alarm, but not injured. Only her dignity and my nerves had been stressed.

I learned to trust her. If she was wet or had gas or was hungry, she cried out, and I grew adept at distinguishing one cry from another. I learned that she did not hold grudges, or let old wounds fester. The lacerating colic that lingered on in my mind disappeared immediately from hers. She had all the instincts of a child outfitted for survival.

However much I came to trust her, I still watched closely. At times, my watchfulness swelled to an overprotective zeal for the job, which, when I saw it in other parents, I found offensive. I realized I would have to learn to let go. But I couldn't do that yet.

One afternoon over a cup of coffee, I confessed as much to Roger. A tall, balding, gregarious man of thirty-one, he took frequent breaks from his job as college admissions director and still worked twelve-hour days.

"Sometimes, I'll be there in the study and I'll start think-

Childcare Mechanics

ing about sudden infant crib death, and I just have to go in there and have a look at her. I get an urge to wake her up to ask her if she's all right."

"Can't you tell by looking at her that she's all right?"

"Well, yes. But the other day I was in there hovering over her and I swear I could not see any sign that she was breathing. The covers weren't moving, I couldn't hear her. No motion beneath the eyelids."

"So you woke her up."

"No, I lowered the side of the crib and bent real low to her face to see if I could feel her breath. I was about an inch away from her face, and then she let out with this huge snort and jabbed her hand up and hit me right on the nose."

Roger laughed. "Just what you deserve. She was telling you to back off."

I smiled at the memory, wondering if Roger could understand what I meant. Could anyone without children of their own understand what I meant?

"Wait until you have a kid, Roger. I bet you'll be a real mother hen, too."

"Probably. But I bet I keep the nest a little cleaner than you do."

From the dining-room table, I followed Roger's gaze across the front door, the bottom of the steps, and into the living room. On ten yards of patchy brown and green carpet, I could have collected an armload of blankets, toys, books, papers, and tennis balls. In the corner behind a shedding Boston fern was a hockey stick.

"Some of those things are Katydog's," I said.

"Oh," said Roger.

"But you're right; the place could use some straightening up. Lillian and I never have had a system for doing housecleaning. It just got done. But it doesn't seem to be getting done anymore, does it?"

DADDY'S HOME

"No," said Roger.

He and Susan kept their house immaculate. Roger not only washed the dishes immediately after dinner, but then dried them and put them away. Nothing was ever left on the kitchen counters.

"I'll have to start in on this place. My folks are coming up for Thanksgiving."

"That's three days. You'd better hire help."

"Nah, I'll get it shaped up."

A clean house was easy. By vacuuming the carpet, dusting, and picking up, the house could be made orderly. A clean house was not what my father and mother were driving three hundred and fifty miles from Akron to see.

They were coming to meet their fifth grandchild. They also wanted to see how their eldest son was faring as a housespouse. My father, especially, was interested in that.

For forty years, my father had made his living as a salesman, using his dark-haired good-looks, his personable manner, and a firm handshake to sell everything from household goods to inventory appraisals. He was proud of my athletic accomplishments, my education, and my career as a journalist. When I wrote for the *Akron Beacon Journal*, the local newspaper, dad was my closest reader, my biggest fan, and woe betide any of his cronies at the Boulevard Tavern who missed anything that appeared under my by-line.

Although he'd never told me of his dismay over my decision to drop out of newspapering, I sensed it in his silences. There was no reason for him to understand why I would want to stay home with a baby; that was women's work. So although he, too, wanted to meet his newest grandchild, I figured he was coming with another purpose as well: He wanted to see if his eldest son was still a man.

Childcare Mechanics

Over the next three days, Lillian and I not only spruced up the house but bought new sheets for the sofa bed and planned two meals, including a traditional turkey dinner. Annie was in good health, Lillian well rested, and I was a confident housespouse. We were ready.

On Thursday morning, I came out of the shower to find Lillian bending over Annie on our bed, applying an ointment to her cheeks.

"Oh, no," I moaned. The rash was back.

"It's not bad."

"Oh, no," I said again. "What luck."

"Your parents won't mind."

"I know, but it just looks so bad. Let's get her a Pocahontas face mask and say it's part of our Thanksgiving observance."

Lillian smiled weakly. She did not find the rash that funny either.

When my mother and father arrived at noon, I suppressed an urge to begin apologizing at the door for Annie's appearance. Hours went by before the subject came up.

"You know, this rash Annie has reminds me of you," said my mother. She is a small woman of wry humor and uncanny sensitivity. She knows what others are thinking and has been able to read me all my life.

"Me?"

"You had this same type of face rash for months."

"Are you kidding me?"

"No. You had bad cradle cap, too. I was embarrassed to take you out for a while."

"I didn't want to be seen with you either," said dad.

"You *are* joking."

"No, I'm not. You were a mess. When my mother came down to Dallas from Pittsburgh on the train for a visit, I was

45

sure she would think me a failure. Because I was *reared* to be a mother."

"And what did she say?"

"She said if I were doing something wrong, I'd know it. Not by a rash, but by a lack of spirit, or energy, or growth. She said a healthy baby cries like he means it."

"Like Annie," I said.

Mom smiled.

The visit seemed to be going well. Dad seemed relaxed; and my mother, after five years between grandchildren, seemed happy to have an infant in her arms once again.

During dinner, Annie sat in her plastic seat on one end of the table, a counterweight to the roast turkey at the other end. Between the pumpkin pie and the coffee, my father asked: "Why does your washing machine always seem to be running?"

"Because it always *is* running," I said.

"But you have a diaper service, don't you?" asked my mother, also puzzled.

"I'm washing the receiving blankets and her clothes. They usually get wet with each diaper."

"Why don't you put plastic pants on her?"

"Diaper rash," I said, surprised that my mother had forgotten about diaper rash.

"Diaper rash?" She didn't understand.

"Yeah. Plastic pants, you know, holding the pee in, cause diaper rash."

"Where did you get that?"

"Read it somewhere."

"Hmmm," she said. "Have you read anything about the cost of a new washing machine? Everybody uses plastic pants. You act like diaper rash is fatal."

"Well . . ."

Childcare Mechanics

On Friday, we bought six pairs of plastic pants and gave the washing machine the day off. The house seemed unusually quiet.

That afternoon, my father and I walked to the college gymnasium. A quilt of blue-gray clouds hung over the campus like a false ceiling. Most students were gone, but the gym was open.

"How's the college team?" For my father, a former four-sport athlete in high school, athletics remained crucial. Our strongest bond had been forged through his instructing me in sports.

"They should be pretty decent this year. Got four starters back, and a six-five freshman. That's big for this league."

We stood in the corner of the gym and watched a short man in green work uniform silently push a broom across the floor.

"This looks like a good gym. Bigger than the one you played in at college."

"Hey, I'm going to play in this one, too, for the faculty-staff team in the intramural league."

He looked at me with happy surprise. "You are? Great! I thought maybe you'd given up basketball."

"Are you kidding? I'm only thirty-five. I've got fifteen years of fast break left in me."

"I'm glad to hear that," said my father, looking genuinely pleased. "I am."

Basketball wasn't all the evidence that my father needed, but it helped. I was a househusband, without a career, a job, and a paycheck, but I was not in a dress, I did not appear effeminate, and I had not given up athletics. I even continued to follow college football, and although I did not consider the Big Ten standings as important as I once had, I kept track. My father could see that caring for a baby had

DADDY'S HOME

not wrought any fundamental changes in character or conduct; his son was still a man.

That night, after a dinner of leftover turkey and gravy, Lillian and I took turns walking Annie up and down the living room, trying to rock her to sleep. At ten o'clock, my mother asked why we didn't just put her in bed.

"She'll cry her head off," I said.

"So?"

"Oh, that colicky scream is unbearable, and she would keep it up forever."

"She doesn't seem to have colic."

Lillian looked at me questioningly. Was she thinking that my mother was becoming officious?

"This is the way we have always put her to sleep, mom. She won't go to sleep if we just put her down."

"Bet?"

"Sure."

We each put in a quarter and wrote down our Estimated Time till Silence on a scrap of paper. Wide awake and suspicious, Annie stared at me all the way upstairs. When I put her down in her crib, she wailed in protest of my betrayal. For the first time in three months, I was actually pleased to hear her cry.

I rejoined the family without making the least attempt to hide the satisfaction I felt. Annie bawled with reassuring vigor. I wondered only that I might have underestimated her endurance: I had predicted forty minutes; maybe I should have upped my guess to an hour.

"Hear that?" I said to mother. "The kid's got lungs of leather." How could she have even *presumed* to know Annie better than I did?

We sat and tried to talk, and waited. The crying seemed to go on forever, but in fifteen minutes it abruptly stopped. My father looked at his watch, opened his squared betting

Childcare Mechanics

slip, spread it on the coffee table, and pocketed the four quarters.

"I don't know why you didn't ask me in the first place," he said to me with a perfectly straight face. "And you thought the only thing I could teach you was how to catch a football!"

Chapter 4

Love and Homemade Adventure

LILLIAN AND I met one afternoon in May in a house on Stanton Street, a short hook of unpaved driveway that dead-ends into a grassy hillside off upper Market in San Francisco. The house had three stories, peeling paint, and a slight eastward bias, evidence that some of its underpinnings were giving way to gravity. I was one of a shifting tide of people who lived there, sharing food, money, and faith, both in the tenacity of the house and in the inevitability of a new social consciousness. They were heady days, back in 1972.

Lillian had just come down to the city after a weekend working on the adobe house that she and several other college friends from Los Angeles had built high in the wil-

Love and Homemade Adventure

derness of Mendocino County. In jeans and hiking boots, her hair pulled back in a ponytail, she looked like almost everybody else who flowed through Stanton Street that year.

I was sitting on the couch trying to make sense of Carlos Castaneda, and getting nowhere, when she and a friend bustled in to have a look at Rick and Carolyn's baby, born a few days earlier. We may have said hi to each other, but no more. I did not pay her much attention.

The next day Lillian called Stan, the taciturn part-time student and accountant who paid the rent on the house, and asked if he and anyone else who happened to be around wanted to go out for a beer. Later, Lillian maintained that she knew that someone else would be me.

Four of us—Lillian; her friend, Fran; Stan and I—spent a Saturday evening at a bar in the Sunset district. Thin and animated, Lillian talked excitedly through the music of an acoustic guitarist about plans to lay a wooden floor in the adobe, about finding someone to help her rebuild the blown engine in her Volkswagen bus, and about the Sturm und Drang of her work at Mendocino State Hospital in Ukiah, where she was a rehabilitation counselor.

On the way to the bar, Stan told me he knew Lillian through a friend who had been a classmate of hers in the master's degree program at California State University at Los Angeles. Stan described her as a former VISTA volunteer, bright, engaging, but, in his words, "too hung up on feminism; she jumps on you if you say anything that even sounds close to being chauvinistic." That did not concern me; in fact, I considered myself a feminist, too.

Halfway through the evening I was sure that Lillian was much too intense for my taste. Her vivacity and energy were infectious. Her green eyes took on such a glow when she talked that I almost felt like running out and building an adobe house myself. She was attractive, interesting, but so

DADDY'S HOME

gung ho! To a professional cynic like me, a little enthusiasm went a long way. Did she ever slow down and relax? I wondered. Had I been looking for romance, I would have thought Fran more my type. Dark-complected where Lillian was fair, she was a former drug abuser who had come through the purgatory of despair with an air of serenity that posed a marked contrast to Lillian's volubility.

I was not particularly looking for romance, however. I was just looking. Four months earlier I had returned from Perth, Australia, after a year as a reporter on a daily tabloid. Although I had relished the casual, suntanned life down under, I had often felt, there on the edge of the world, too far away from the action. The climate in San Francisco suited me—both the bright blue coolness that swirled around the hills, and the vibrant freakiness that ran along the streets. Not only did I have friends in the Bay Area, but I knew I could support myself as a free-lance writer, and not have to hunt for a full-time newspaper job. With a place to stay, a source of income, and no attachments or obligations, I felt comfortably disengaged.

I did not know that I had fallen in love with Lillian until a week later, when she told me. We had come back tired and hungry from an afternoon of hiking on Mount Tamalpais in Marin County. We were standing under the blue gum eucalyptus trees in front of the house as we waited for the group to reassemble for dinner somewhere.

"Why are you so sarcastic all the time?" Lillian asked. "Are you afraid of me?"

I picked up a handful of buttonlike seeds and began tossing them distractedly at the base of a tree. I felt like a chastised schoolboy. "No," I managed to say. Her directness had surprised me. I felt uncomfortable, not only because of

Love and Homemade Adventure

her ingenuousness but because I recognized the implication of what she asked. I *had* been sarcastic toward her, trying to be witty. I wanted to impress her with the same ironic detachment I used as a safety net between me and genuine involvement. "I just have a weird sense of humor, I guess."

"Well, sometimes you're funny. But I get the feeling you've been picking on me, coming on too strong."

"I'm sorry."

"I'm interested in you. I mean, I got the impression somewhere that we might—get together."

I looked up at her, silently cheering. She was not flushed. She stood with her hands in her back pockets, smiling expectantly, without hint of embarrassment or contrivance. She was soon to return to Ukiah, and she wanted to know if indeed I had been flirting with her in some bizarre, contradictory way.

Yes, of course I had been flirting with her, in a way that served to confuse even myself.

"Yes," I said, with an unexpected sense of relief. "I think we might."

That night, after Lillian had gone, I began to realize what had happened. I sat smiling to myself, listening to a Stevie Wonder record, feeling like the sole possessor of the key to enlightenment. I did not appreciate then that what I had seen under the eucalyptus trees was the soul of Lillian's nature. She did not abide pretense or deception, or guile or phoniness; and in calling me out of a tired game I did not even realize I was playing, she had cut to the heart of the matter. The prospect of beginning a romance with someone who was at once so disarmingly candid and mysteriously different filled me with anticipation. I was an excitable seven-year-old on Christmas eve.

We met the next weekend, and the weekend after that, and then began to figure out how we could arrange a merger of our lives. Within weeks Lillian had requested a transfer to a vacancy in the San Francisco office of the state Rehabilitation Department, and in July we rented a home that only a hillside city can offer: a basement apartment with a panoramic view out the back.

Lillian paid the rent and bought the food while I tried to keep myself in pocket money by free-lancing magazine articles to the city's two daily newspapers, the *Chronicle* and *Examiner*. At the same time I held on to an irregular, unremunerative, but fascinating job writing Elvis Presley fan club bulletins ("The Hound Dogger"), advertising copy, film scripts, and personal correspondence for a Sausalito man with a warehouse full of old teen-age fan magazines and a million fanciful ideas about growing rich.

One day in the summer of 1973, Lillian came home from the office as discouraged as I had ever seen her.

"What happened?"

"Everything. Bobby, my transsexual client, overdosed after a fight with her boyfriend. She'll probably have to miss her sex-change operation, maybe forever. My suicidal paraplegic lost his job at the sheltered workshop. I think he can hang on, but I'm worried. The district supervisor just announced that our case loads are being increased to one hundred fifteen, and added that we should be making twelve closures a month. And Roz is quitting to go to work for a bank. How's that?"

"Damn," I said.

Lillian fell dejectedly into our one chair, a huge foam-filled pillow that she had made from upholstery scraps. She stared out the window toward the houses of Daly City, the "little boxes made of ticky-tacky" in Malvina Reynolds's famous song. After dark, the lights would turn the tight rows of boxes into "strings of pearls" around the hills, but now they just looked depressing.

Love and Homemade Adventure

"Maybe it's time for a change," said Lillian.
"What are you thinking of?"
"School. I was talking to an old professor from Cal State today about Ph.D. programs. I think I'd rather teach than work much longer with street crazies."

The implication of Lillian's returning to school was immediately apparent. I would have to find a job—a full-time, living-wage job. I liked the idea. I was ready for a change, too.

Although money had not caused any serious dissension between us, neither Lillian nor I ever forgot that it was she who paid the bills. She carried me without complaint or condescension; but the more checks I wrote for typing paper or groceries, the more I began to wish that I had put half the money in the bank. Lillian had never known me as a reporter employed full-time. The image of me with a steady job, and a weekly paycheck in my name, rapidly grew in appeal.

"The only place I am fairly certain I could get a job is in Akron at the *Beacon Journal.*"
"Do you want to go back there?"
"It's a good paper. I wouldn't mind."
"And your folks?"
"They would love to have us nearby. But we won't live next door."

After a series of phone calls and letters, we spent Lillian's vacation on a cross-country trip to Ohio, where I talked to the newspaper's editors and she talked to the graduate-school faculty at Kent State University, twenty miles east of Akron. Two weeks later, when we drove westward, it was to get ready to move. Lillian would be admitted to the doctoral program at Kent, and I would return to the newsroom where eight years earlier I had unsuspectingly stumbled into a trade from which an English major could fashion a career.

DADDY'S HOME

As a graduate student in literature at Kent State in 1965, I had been more interested in maintaining my student deferment from the draft than I was in the sprung rhythm of Gerard Manley Hopkins. At twenty-two, I was a prime candidate for the voracious military machine then growing larger and sinking deeper into the distant swamp of Vietnam.

My parents encouraged any licit means through which I could avoid the draft, but after putting me through four expensive years at Beloit College in Wisconsin they were unable to maintain my checking account indefinitely. They thought it time I went to work.

Like thousands of other English majors confronted with the commercial impracticality of their scholastic training, I vaguely thought I would continue being a student until I fell into a teaching job somewhere. I thought teaching still my most probable vocation when I took a job with the *Beacon Journal* as a city desk clerk for the money to pay another quarter's tuition, buy books, and rent a small furnished apartment.

After graduation from Beloit, I had lugged home a boxful of poems, short stories, and plays, along with the conviction that I had the soul of an artist. But I had never considered writing for a newspaper. Under my still-wet artistic credo, I was not sure that the prose of newspaper reporters qualified as writing.

Almost immediately I began to see not only that good reporters did indeed write, but that they wrote quickly, clearly, and concisely, and that their abilities paid them a living wage. The pressure of looming deadlines, the pounding urgency of the reporter's style, the diversity of subjects, the daily reward of publication—all of this struck me as an exciting, demanding, and yet socially useful way to spend the day.

Love and Homemade Adventure

As impressed as I was with the realization that there was space in the newspaper for writers, I was equally taken with the genial air of self-confidence and wry humor that reporters seemed to affect. The volatility, the hurried pace, the ironic detachment of newspeople, even the cigarette smoke, commingled in an atmosphere that to me seemed just right. In the newsroom I saw how ill-suited to academia I was. Most of the professors I knew were too stuffy, too placid, or too remote. Reporters and editors, I realized, were either more like me or more like I wanted to be.

I began writing club announcements, and obituaries, and the daily weather summary, and cajoled reporters to toss me their leftovers, the little tidbits they would not have time to work up for print. I seized on any material I thought I could tease into a story and get in the paper. When I had been there six months, I persuaded the city editor, Bruce McIntyre, to make me a reporter. He assigned me to the police beat, and my salary went from $85 a week to $90.50, union scale for first-year journalists.

Graduate school no longer interested me. I dropped out of Kent State, and lost my student deferment. Several weeks later, just ahead of the draft board, McIntyre, who was also a captain in the army reserve, found a haven for me in his intelligence unit. I would escape Vietnam.

Eight years later, in August 1973, we headed back to Ohio, this time with our aging Volkswagen packed to the roof. I was sure I could avoid the traps of going home again by expecting everything to be different. And it was. Although I was returning to the same newspaper, and the same job as a general-assignment reporter, I was different. I was older, and I was more experienced, having worked in England, the Bahamas, Australia. I felt sure of my craft, confident that I could write tight, solid news stories on the shortest of deadlines. Moreover, I had in Lillian a partner who settled me, who gave me more to think about than just a career or adventure or the aimless pursuit of some image of what a journalist's life should be. She gave me a responsibility beyond myself, a reassuring weight, and the certainty that there was more to the day than the brief intoxication of a front-page by-line and a celebratory drink afterward.

We rented a small house surrounded by cornfields halfway between Akron and Kent, plowed up a plot for next spring's garden, and adopted an irrepressible black and white puppy we called Katydog. Lillian studied educational statistics and psychology, heading off to Kent each day wearing a green backpack filled with thick books and papers on chi-square analysis and regression theory. She made some money as a graduate assistant, advising students on research projects, but now I paid the rent and bought the food on my journeyman reporter's salary of $340 a week. After the penury of San Francisco, the money was a welcome weight in my pocket.

For three years Lillian drove the fifteen miles into Kent, boring closer and closer toward her Ph.D., and I commuted into Akron, covering labor strikes and traffic smashups and writing feature stories about tiny, endangered fish and about people with huge problems for two hundred thousand subscribers in the Rubber Capital of the world.

By the time Lillian finished her dissertation (on the gender of generic pronouns and its effects on identification and memory) and I had driven the back road into Akron about as many times as I could stand, we were both ready for change again. For me, the weekly paycheck was no longer novelty enough. Lillian wanted to start working, and I wanted to stop. While she investigated jobs in counseling and research, I applied for one of twenty-four journalism fellowships offered by the National Endowment for the Humanities at either the University of Michigan or Stanford University.

Love and Homemade Adventure

In the spring of 1976, Lillian came back from a two-day interview for an administrative job at Bexley College in Michigan and told me that the toughest question put to her during her visit was why she and I were not married.

"How did that come up?" I scowled, envisioning some prying panel of small-town conservatives tsk-tsking over our morals.

"Awkwardly," said Lillian. "I wanted to mention you so that, if we do go there, you won't be a surprise. I said I'm not married, but I live with someone. The provost asked me how long we had lived together. When I said four years, he said: 'Why don't you get married then?' I told him there never seemed to be any reason to get married. But it sounded lame."

We looked at each other in silence, thinking of the same obvious remedy.

"Maybe we should," I said.

"Who knows what the people in a small town will be like?" agreed Lillian. "They won't be like San Francisco, or even Akron."

"If we go there, maybe we should."

By mid-May, Lillian had accepted a position as counselor at Bexley College, to begin in June, and I had been awarded a fellowship at the University of Michigan. In September I would start spending the week in Ann Arbor. I quit the *Beacon Journal* for the second time, and although the editor who had hired me said I would be welcomed back when the fellowship ended, I knew I would not be back. The program Lillian had been hired to evaluate was scheduled to run for three years, and I was sure that I needed more than a year away from the newsroom and the chafing of the clock.

Before going to Michigan, we decided to take the awk-

DADDY'S HOME

wardness out of the introductions to come. I would become Lillian's husband, as in "This is my husband, Mike," and she would become my wife, as in "My wife works at the college."

On a gentle Saturday afternoon, the fourth anniversary of our first meeting, we stood under a canopy of maple leaves in my parents' backyard and were married by a Presbyterian minister, a family friend. Although neither Lillian nor I professed any particular religion, we had both been raised as Protestants, and in front of a small group of family and friends we repeated the vows from the Book of Common Worship after changing the "men" into "people."

Our belongings no longer fit into the Volkswagen. We packed a U-Haul truck with our bed, three chairs, a small couch, and several hundred pounds of books, and with a tranquilized Katydog moved to Michigan in the first week of June. We found a house near campus, Lillian walked to work, and I threw myself into learning the neighborhood, our neighbors, some new recipes, and the Detroit Tigers, by position and batting average. It was a grand summer; I discovered several tennis partners, and the Tigers discovered Mark Fidrych.

We did not begin talking about a child right away, but I began thinking about it. Casually, we had discussed children even before we were married. We liked children. My brother and sister, and Lillian's sister, already had children, and we liked them. We thought we would like to have a child when the time was right.

On the road between home and Ann Arbor, I thought about my age. I was thirty-three. If a child were born right then, I thought, I would be thirty-eight when he or she started kindergarten, forty-eight in the first year of high school, fifty-four by college graduation. I wondered if the generation gap was already too wide. My father had been

Love and Homemade Adventure

only twenty-nine when I was born, and I recalled that by the time I was fourteen he couldn't catch my fast ball anymore.

Lillian was twenty-nine. The older she got, the more dangerous childbirth would become.

I thought the time was right, but getting later in a hurry.

Over the summer, in bits and pieces, we had a conversation about children. Compressed into one continuous dialogue, the whole discussion did not take long. And it always led us to the same conclusion.

"I think we should have a kid," I would say.

"I like kids," Lillian would say.

"Good. Let's have one."

"When?"

"Now."

"It takes longer than that. It takes planning."

"Let's start now."

"What happens when the baby arrives?"

"We feed and clothe it, give it a bath, play with it," I would say. "Raise it."

"Who will?" Lillian would ask.

"We will."

"Together?"

"Yes, of course."

"Who is going to be earning the money to buy the food and clothes, and who is going to be at home doing the playing and bathing?"

"Both of us."

"But who is going to do what, in which order?"

"What do you want to do?"

"I want to spend the next three years working full-time."

"So you don't want the bathing-and-playing part?"

"Not as a full-time housewife. I would go crazy."

That was true. Though I was not sure exactly what housewives did all day, I was sure that Lillian was not cut out to be one. She was too energetic, too dependent on the stimulation of people and activity to spend her days at home. She liked to set goals, to get involved in complex projects, to work as a member of a team. She had not earned a Ph.D. just to become a mother.

"We could hire someone to care for the baby," Lillian would say. "With two full-time jobs, we could certainly afford help."

That was also true. But somehow the idea of handing our baby over to someone else to care for struck me as unnecessary. For many couples, economics or temperament made childcare help essential. But I was uncomfortable with the implication that we were too busy, or that we did not want to get involved until our son or daughter could hold up one end of a converstion, or play ball.

Moreover, I did not want to spend another year commuting, living apart from Lillian and our child, and there was no newspaper that I wanted to work for even if a job were available. In fact, I was not ready to submit to a five-day-a-week work schedule at all.

That left me to mention the third option.

"I could stay home and take care of the baby," I said—and when the words came out, they made me imagine a daring adventure, full of promise.

"You could," Lillian said, and she meant it.

By the time the fall term had begun, we had stopped preventing the conception of a child, and I was sure that if Lillian were to become pregnant, I would become a househusband. Once that notion had settled in me as naturally as my faith that we would have a baby, I wondered how the arrangement could ever have been any different. And of course, it could not have been.

Love and Homemade Adventure

Despite my support of feminist principles even before meeting Lillian, her influence had deepened my belief that women's liberation would not only help free women from the tyranny of sexism but would also free men. If I stayed home with a baby, Lillian would escape the baby trap, and perhaps refute the conventional wisdom that a woman *had* to handle the first two years of infancy.

For me, the potential for social statement was even greater. The risk of failure was greater, too. But here, unmistakably, was a chance to prove my commitment to change, to put up or shut up. Again, Lillian had helped me shuck my tendency to stay on the sidelines, the reporter's habitual position, and get involved. Like most men and boys, I had lived a full imaginary life of masculine adventures, many on an epic scale. But here, in the safety and comfort of my own home, came an invitation to what would prove to be my most daring exploit yet. And this risky enterprise would prove to be real.

I could not have chosen to stay home only as a dramatic gesture on behalf of men's and women's liberation. I was neither martyr nor fanatic nor domestic daredevil. I wanted to stay home because housespousing sounded like a challenge, like fun, like a convenient way to vote for change, to be different, to avoid going back to work for wages.

More important, my staying home was the only way that we might have a child soon. And I wanted to have a child. I thought I was ready to be more than just a newspaper reporter, or a husband, or a weekend jock, bird watcher, gardener, or a healthy blue-eyed man with a charmed life and a longing for something else. I was ready to take on responsibility for more than myself, to be more than just a man. I was ready to become a father.

Chapter 5

The Baby Mixer

MEN did not attend showers. Showers were women's affairs. Men went to parties, or stag nights, or beer blasts, or smokers, but not showers.

So when Susan told me that I was not only expected to attend the shower she was giving but that I would be a guest of honor, I reacted like any man would. I said no.

"Don't be a jerk," said Susan, who never minced words. "Everything else connected with this baby is different, so why not this?"

"But a shower . . ." I protested weakly.

"You'll be using the gifts more than Lillian. Why shouldn't you be there to accept them, too?"

The Baby Mixer

"Well," I allowed, "I hadn't thought about it." I really hadn't. "Are you going to invite other men?"

"Of course. Just like any party. Think of it as a mixer."

A "mixer" was a good name for the party I imagined. Fourteen friends, most of them married couples and all associated with the college, would gather over the usual assortment of drinks and snacks at Roger and Susan Vander's house to celebrate the impending birth of our child, due three weeks later, in mid-August. I expected the party would be like any of the half-dozen other parties we had attended in the past year: College politics and personalities would provide the bulk of the conversational fodder; the tone would range from moderate hum to occasional roar; and at about 11:30, when the food was gone and scattered yawns were breaking out, everyone would go home.

Despite the occasion for the party, I did not expect any of the guests to spend much time discussing with us our unconventional plans for childcare. They never had. The only person we had talked with at length about our plans, and who shared our eager anticipation of putting them into practice, was Susan. Since she had become an administrator of a nearby city, and almost immediately begun dreaming of bigger cities to run, her career had pulled even with Roger's in prestige, income, and importance. For Susan, a tall blonde whose easy sardonic humor did not conceal an intense competitive drive, hosting the shower was a way she could express an emotional investment in us. She did not want to rule out becoming a mother herself, but, like Lillian, she was not about to sacrifice her career to become a full-time housewife. Out loud, she hoped that our example might become an alternative for them.

"I want you to make caring for the baby look irresistibly masculine," she kidded me.

DADDY'S HOME

"I'll be the Tom Sawyer of the nursery," I promised. "Roger will be begging for a job like mine."

We both knew that it would take more than me to induce Roger to become a househusband. Perhaps no one enjoyed his job more than Roger. As the person responsible for keeping the college filled with students, he operated like a charismatic preacher, knowing just when to be businessman, jokester, or pal. He was never more in his element than when conducting a group of high-school seniors and their parents on a tour of the campus. Impeccably turned out, and at six-foot-four towering over the knot of tourists surrounding him, Roger mixed solemnity and laughter to sell the college and himself. Where I looked forward to time alone with a sleeping child, Roger would go stir crazy.

On a hot, starry evening in late July, the guests arrived two to a package. Once in the door, the women carried their gifts to the coffee table and joined the other women. The mothers in the group took turns offering recollections of pregnancy as Lillian shifted her weight around in a straight chair in a vain search for comfort.

The men headed for the kitchen, where they grabbed bottles of beer from the refrigerator and leaned back against the counter to choose between an analysis of the Tigers' midseason slump or a debate on the college's influence on the city commission.

By my third beer I realized that this shower we called a "mixer" was not like any other party at all. It was turning out to be the most rigidly sex-segregated affair I had ever attended.

"No one is mixing at this mixer," I whispered to Susan when she crashed the kitchen for more dip and cauliflower. "This reminds me of compulsory dance class in the sixth grade."

The Baby Mixer

"You come into the living room and start opening gifts with Lillian. I'll herd these guys in."

I pulled up a chair next to Lillian, who looked hot and enormous in a green dress that flared around her belly. Susan yelled, "Party time! Let's see what the baby got!"

As we confronted the gift-wrapped mound at our feet, an odd air of tension seemed to descend around us. At first it seemed quiet. The men restlessly milled around the living room. The women shifted uneasily in their seats. Then Roger began asking if everyone had a drink, and Joan loudly inquired what shower games we were going to play.

"We could see how many different words we can make out of 'househusband,' " Joan suggested.

"That would take all night," laughed another woman.

"What are shower games?" demanded someone in the back.

"How about 'dry nurse'?" suggested someone else.

I did not mind being the center of attention; in fact, I usually delighted in a chance to star. But on the brink of my baptismal shower, I wondered if I could find something appropriate to say about the presents we were about to reveal. I felt responsible for any awkward silences, and, as we began opening gifts, I tried to fill them up.

"Okay, now, you're going to have to help me with this. What is the custom in your country? Cards first? All right. Says here, 'Dearest Michael, I have missed you so much, my darling, since we last met. . . .' Hey, how did that get in here!"

It quickly became apparent that my monologue would not be necessary. Everyone was ready to loosen up; the laughs came easily. As Lillian and I took turns displaying knitted sweater-and-cap sets, rattles, stuffed animals, and tasseled booties, the women who clustered tightly around us laid down a steady stream of commentary and exclamation. I felt relieved, and, as the hubbub over the gifts increased, I began thoroughly to enjoy my inaugural baby shower.

"Oh, Connie! That's beautiful," cooed Ruth over an embroidered quilt I stood to unfold.

"It is," I added, echoing Ruth's effusive tone. "Did you do this by hand?"

"Well, I used a machine," said Connie, flushed with pleasure over the reaction her handiwork had caused. "I copied the pattern from the shower invitation."

"Oh, you *did!*" Joan said rapturously. "It's gorgeous."

Soon the women began passing along useful tips on infantcare, like one mother to another. Lillian fielded some, but others were directed at me.

"You can't have too many of these lounge suits," Ruth advised earnestly. "When Jennifer was a baby, these were the only things she wore. Sleeping, daytime, whenever."

"Wow! Fifteen minutes ago I had never even heard of lounge suits," I confessed.

"You'll get to be very familiar with them, believe me."

"And you want to stick with this type that has the snaps down the leg," Giselle pointed out. "You can change a diaper without having to undress the baby."

"You can avoid getting poop all over everything, too," added Ruth confidentially.

"Good," I said, all sincerity. "That's just the sort of thing I want to avoid."

Up to my ankles in wrapping paper, I realized what a good time I was having. There had developed between me and the women around me a genuine bond. They were sisters in the sorority of motherhood, and, as much as Lillian, I was being rushed. As a prospective member of their club, they showered me with attention, and heaped on the practical advice. They had accepted me as an earnest pledge, a seeker on the perimeter of their inner circle.

The Baby Mixer

Yet I was aware of an outer circle behind the women, a restive ring of men hovering warily on the fringes of the party. George was the only man even to sit down, and he was thumbing through *Newsweek*.

I tried to pull in the brothers. "John," I called, "what do you think of this?" I held up a tiny yellow shirt emblazoned with a Disney duckling.

John, a strapping, athletic math professor, was standing with two other men behind the couch. He appeared almost startled. "I think if you can get into it, you'll be cute as the dickens," he said.

Eager laughter burst out everywhere as the guests turned to look at John in appreciation. But despite his wide grin, he looked ready to bolt. His eyes moved from face to face, and he took a halting step toward the kitchen.

Where had I seen that quiet distress before?

Of course; I had seen that look on the faces of our fathers —mine and Lillian's—right after we told them about the baby, when it became clear just what that baby would mean.

We had flown to the San Joaquin Valley of California for Christmas, and when Lillian's nausea hung on too long to be airsickness or the abrupt change in climate, she delivered a urine sample to a medical laboratory in Lindsay.

"Yippee!" I shouted as we drove the right-angle route around square fields of citrus trees to Bill and Nancy Buchanan's orange grove, fast against the foothills of the Sierras. "We are with child!"

Ranks of mourning doves sleepily sunned themselves on the power lines and with one eye watched us pass by. Under an azure sky, I felt filled with energy and light-headed with prosperity. I leaned over to kiss the expectant mother, and the car veered toward an irrigation ditch. Lillian lunged for the steering wheel.

DADDY'S HOME

"We are in danger if you don't calm down," she said, looking serious.

Chastened, I returned both hands to the wheel. "Sorry. But I am pretty high on the idea of having a kid."

"So am I," Lillian said. "But I want us all in one piece. Including you. You're not *just* going to become a father, you know. You're going to become a father with a child to take care of."

I spent little time trying to imagine what my days as a househusband would be like. The role of father was the part that thrilled me; my caring for the baby seemed merely an inviting consequence, a secondary adventure.

When we burst into the kitchen with the news, the reaction of Lillian's parents mirrored mine. The promise of a third grandchild was the aspect of pregnancy they found important.

"That's wonderful," beamed Nancy. "I was hoping to hear an announcement like this soon." She hugged her daughter proudly.

Lillian was twenty-nine. I was five years older. Was that what she meant—that we were getting old?

"When is this baby due?" asked Bill, a trim, hardworking man who had turned to farming after an early retirement as a government engineer. He was sitting at the kitchen table.

"August."

"August. What will you do then?"

"I'll stay home for a couple of years, and then Lillian will probably stay home while I go back to work," I said as matter-of-factly as I could.

Bill nodded, mulling it over. If he found my plan to become a househusband an admirable prospect, he might have said as much. But he remained silent.

From the chinaberry tree next to the house I heard the

70

The Baby Mixer

tremolo of an oriole. Nancy turned back to the sink. "Wonderful. I'll have to start knitting."

Two days later we repeated the announcement in a living room in Ohio. I sank into the couch, trying to ignore a headache, relieved that a twelve-hour day of sitting in airplanes, airports, and cars was over. Outside in the dark, the wind slanted a snowy drizzle into the picture window, ice pinging off the glass.

My father had kissed Lillian, and shaken my hand with his characteristically firm grip. "Congratulations, Mike," he said warmly, father to son.

He settled into a recliner. "August, huh?"

"We figure about mid-August. But that's just a guess."

"Oh, I'm so happy for you," said mother, setting down a plate of cheese and crackers. "Do you think you could arrange to have a boy? We've got three granddaughters, but only one grandson."

"I think the order has already been placed," said Lillian.

"We'll be happy either way. Now what about your work, Lillian?" my mother asked.

"I'm going to finish the project at Alma at least. That's three years. Then I'll probably stay home for a while and Mike can go back to work."

Once again the conversation lapsed into silence. Dad stared off to my left, his limpid blue eyes giving away nothing. I listened for the sound of the oriole in the chinaberry tree, and heard instead the shrill wind gust against the window.

"How do you think he'll do as a househusband?" Lillian cheerfully jumped in.

"Oh, I think he'll do fine," mother said, lingering over the "fine." "All he has to do is follow my example. Look how *he* turned out." She winked at me conspiratorily.

DADDY'S HOME

My father blinked and allowed a smile to develop at the corners of his mouth.

We talked about the warm weather in central California while we finished our drinks. Then we trudged upstairs to bed.

In many ways Lillian's parents and mine were alike. All four were about sixty years of age, and shared a conservative, middle-American traditionalism that comes easily to people who grew up during the Depression. They valued hard work and industry, and encouraged ambition. They held, in short, to the Protestant ethic, and tried to pass that belief in self-improvement along to their children.

Our mothers, both named Nancy, were practical, sensitive women, accustomed to sacrifice for their children and their husbands. Living with provident but volatile men—both products of impoverished childhoods—they often kept the peace by holding their tongues. To our minds, they did not have liberated marriages, but they had grown comfortable with their partnerships.

Our parents would no longer presume to tell us what to do. They might offer approval, or they might offer silence, but they had recognized years ago that we were past the age of obedience. Even if they believed it to be true, Lillian's parents would not tell their son-in-law that becoming a househusband was foolish. They could only trust their daughter's judgment, and have faith that we were not off course. Neither would my parents try to dissuade me from a decision so personal and so central to our lives, however odd they believed it to be. Before Lillian and I were married, my mother had asked "how best to describe" our live-in relationship. My father had remarked that he hoped to see me in short hair and with a clean-shaven face before he died, and he did not bother to smile when he said it. But they kept

The Baby Mixer

their own counsel. They did not attempt to interfere in our lives.

At that Saturday-night shower, my decision to become a househusband was too personal and too unwieldy for casual discussion. Later we were to see our friends deal with the subject as our parents had: They ignored it.

The baby shower ended even before the beer ran out.

"I thought it went pretty well," said Roger. He was briskly straightening up the kitchen while Lillian and Susan collected glasses, bottles, and empty plates. I packed gifts into a large cardboard box.

"Yeah, for a party that never got off the ground, it skimmed right along," Susan sighed.

"What do you mean?" Roger came out of the kitchen wearing an apron and a look of amazement. "I had a great time. I think everybody enjoyed it."

"It was stiff. Only half the guests really took part," said Susan, her voice rising. "I don't think Peter Dodge came out of the kitchen all night."

"Well, he was enjoying himself. So what?"

"So this was a baby shower. We were opening gifts out here."

"Men don't know how to act at a baby shower. They've never been to one before." Roger dismissed Susan's complaint with a laugh. "What do you expect?"

"I expected that everyone *at* the party would take part in the party," said Susan. She turned to Lillian. "Know what Mattie said to me on her way out? 'Well, it's just odd enough to work, but I sure couldn't imagine John staying home with the baby.'"

"Not our baby," I said.

"Not even one of their babies," said Lillian.

Susan remained annoyed. "It just bugs me to hear that

kind of snide comment," she said. "Like they're hoping you'll fail."

"No, I don't think it's that," said Lillian. "It's just that the subject of kids is one that everyone has an opinion about."

"Yeah, even people who don't have kids have opinions," said Roger, grinning impishly. "Like me. I think all children should be sent to military boarding school at the age of six."

Susan rolled her eyes, unable to hide her amusement. "See what I'm up against?" she asked us.

"Who knows what to do with kids?" I said. "Our only hope is that ours will come with instructions."

"You have to do what's sensible, right?" said Susan. "I mean, you two are simply going to do what's most convenient."

Lillian laughed. "And like Mattie said, it may just be odd enough to work."

I tucked a koala bear into a corner of the box and spread the quilt over everything. "I'll shove this box and the car seat over there in the corner and pick it up tomorrow, all right? We're walking."

We thanked our friends and began following the paved trail across campus. Our house was about three blocks away.

The summer air was heavy with the perfume of the linden trees in bloom all along the walk past the chapel. In the distance I could hear the 10:45 freight to Midland grind through town, its cars banging roughly into each other as it slowed for the turn past the Tastee Freeze. Closer by, from behind a screened window in a dormitory room, Bob Seger sang about practicing his "night moves" in the back seat of a '60 Chevy. Had Lillian not been tired and logy and burdened with the eighth month of pregnancy, I might have suggested we idle a while on the grass.

"Do you think what we're doing is 'convenient'?"

The Baby Mixer

"Hmmm," said Lillian, giving the syllable a pensive twist of skepticism.

"No?"

"It probably seems convenient. It suits *us*. We are each going to do what we want to do. We don't have to move. But I don't think it's convenient for others."

"What does it have to do with others? We're the ones having the kid."

"But by doing something different, we'll be reminding people that the traditional way is not the only way," said Lillian.

We held hands, and walked the rest of the way home without speaking.

That night I lay awake in bed and recalled how rapidly I had shed any misgivings I had had about being baby-showered, the trappings of infancy piling up around me. I had enjoyed myself, I had enjoyed making a bold declaration of my new role, flaunting my iconoclastic intent. I smiled to myself at the small-town notoriety I had gained—and the baby was not even born yet.

I liked the novelty of my position. And our arrangement did suit us. Lillian could continue to work, and I could stay home. When the baby did not need me, I could write. It was convenient.

Or was it?

Was it really convenient for us to lead lives so radically different from those around us, our families and our friends? While delighting in the jokes I'd made over gifts like food warmers and teddy bears, clearly my role as a prospective househusband caused many of our friends at the party to squirm. To many people we represented a rebuke, a personal affront to their values, as if by rejecting convention in our own way of living we were criticizing the way they lived.

After the baby was born, I supposed, we would become

even more different, grow even more strange to our family and friends. But what else could we do? We might be considered mavericks or heretics or incomprehensible kooks, but we would have to learn to live with that. It was, after all, *our* life, *our* baby.

Chapter 6

A Gently Terrific Birth

WHEN we had been in the delivery room for two hours and the baby had still not come out, I began silently to name the fear that had lurked in the back of my mind all day: death.

I had been thinking that either Lillian or the baby might be in danger of dying. It scared me.

"Jim, what is happening?" Our doctor, small, boyish-looking, was dressed in baggy light green. He looked strange. A soft-spoken, witty man, I knew him both as our family physician and a friend. I knew him best as a quick, clever guard on the basketball team on which we both played.

"Contractions aren't strong enough," he said in the same calm, matter-of-fact way he said everything.

DADDY'S HOME

"They feel strong," said Lillian.

"The baby's coming. I think the head just needs to get around the coccyx. Don't bear down until I tell you."

I looked at the watch in my hand. In ten seconds another contraction would begin. "Get ready," I told Lillian.

She started puffing, blowing out air like Moby Dick.

"One, two, three, pant, pant, pant, pant. Big breath, in, hold it . . . and let it go."

Lillian pulled back on the pistol-grip handles of the delivery table, pushed on the stirrups with her legs, and, as the wave of peristalsis swept through her body with a shudder, emitted a low moan.

"Baby's crowning," said Jim. "I can see the head now." He pointed to a dark spot in the mirror, a circle of matted hair amid the confusion of blood and pink tissue between Lillian's legs. "That's the top of your baby," he said. "That's good work."

"Yeah, I can see it," said Lillian. "We're moving, aren't we?"

We were moving, but not fast enough to quell my anxiety. The mild contractions that had signaled the beginning of this birth had come well before we checked into the hospital at seven in the morning. It was now more than fourteen hours later. I was tired. I was convinced that what had come advertised as one of life's rhapsodic epiphanies was about to fall apart into a medical emergency.

I looked around the small delivery room of the hundred-bed community hospital. Two nurses, Jim, and a young fourth-year medical student all stood staring at Lillian's vagina like a group of construction engineers contemplating an unexpected problem that had cropped up in the foundation of a new house.

We were all tired. But was anyone as worried as I was? I looked at these people in the same way that I look at

A Gently Terrific Birth

flight attendants after I hear a strange noise in an airplane. Is there any sign of alarm? Are they blowing up the life rafts? What are they talking about?

Our crew didn't seem to be talking much at all. They were merely waiting. Jim backed up, leaned against the wall, and closed his eyes, a drained expression of fatigue on his face. One nurse maintained the same vacant half-smile she had come in with, while the other took a seat on a stool near the delivery table and stared blankly, nonchalant to the point of boredom. The student left the room, saying something about wanting to see how they were doing in the delivery room next door.

Was I the only one who appreciated the seriousness of our situation?

Standing at Lillian's head, holding her hand, I could look in the round mirror at the end of the table and almost believe I was watching a television monitor on which was being shown actual film of a very slow birth. The mirror, and the white gown that covered Lillian from her neck to her knees, seemed to disconnect us from the blood and the tissue, and gave the scene a secondhand remoteness.

But that blood was Lillian's. It was she being cut into, opened wider, parted down the middle. Three times Jim had made incisions to enlarge the opening, and these episiotomies had completely severed the bridge of flesh between the vagina and the rectum. There seemed nothing between all of us and Lillian's innards.

So why didn't the baby come out?

"How are you feeling?" I asked her again. I was seeking reassurance, asking her to calm me down. I wanted some clue as to whether she shared my apprehension.

"Fine," she said, almost spryly. "Tired, but fine."

She did not sound concerned, but I was afraid for her anyway. The longer the baby held out, I thought, the greater

DADDY'S HOME

the chances that she would have to undergo a cesarean section. That was a major operation, requiring a major revision in the script of the natural, benign drama for which we had rehearsed.

With a quickened appreciation for the danger Lillian was in, I wanted to take over. Watching the might of the contractions that gripped her body, I wanted to take her place. "Here, let me," I wanted to say. "Let me in there on the table. I'll bear this pain."

I feared that perhaps Lillian was not going to prove strong enough for the ordeal the birth had become. This was hard, demanding, physical work. This was something a man should do.

I had prepared for childbirth. I had taken the classes, read the books, seen the movie. I knew there would be blood. I am not squeamish. I was ready for some deviation from the textbook model. But I was not prepared to see Lillian under stress for so long, to see her work so hard. And I was surprised that she could withstand this long trial with so much grit.

I thought of our weekly Lamaze classes, our instruction in prepared childbirth, and our diligent practice of the breathing exercises and cadenced counting that we had been using for hours. I recalled the sight of ten couples, all on the floor in the First Presbyterian Church each Thursday evening, the men on their knees, the women supine, their great bellies in the air. There on the carpeted floor of the church Fellowship Hall we men confronted the swollen realization of the one task we could never perform ourselves. Perhaps Fernand Lamaze dreamed up a role for men because he recognized and sympathized with our superfluousness. We were called "coaches," but we were really cheerleaders. We could urge the women on, but we could not take over.

In the delivery room, the perspective was familiar, but the

A Gently Terrific Birth

sense of ineffectualness was magnified. I could swab Lillian's forehead with a cool washcloth, rub her back, tell her that I loved her. But I could not muscle that child out into the world.

"How are you feeling?" Lillian asked me. "You must be getting tired, too."

Me? She was asking about me? I was exhausted. My back ached, hunger clawed at my stomach, and my eyeballs felt like they were being massaged by a crosscut saw. I wanted to lie down, anywhere.

"Okay," said Jim when another dozen powerful contractions had pushed a little more of the baby's head into the mirror. "I'm going to try to get forceps in there."

My God! I thought when I saw the size of the silver tongs the smiling nurse laid at Jim's hand. The film of childbirth we had seen two weeks earlier in the last Lamaze class had shown nothing like this. That birth had been so easy, so uncomplicated. There had been no mention of forceps.

The next forty-five minutes passed in blurry slow motion. The overhead lights bounced off the cold glare of the instruments and machinery, combining with the whites and pastels of the uniforms to give everything a trancelike, dreamworld unreality. The steady blip-blip of the heart monitor, the faint hum of the nurses' rubber-soled shoes, Lillian's crescendoing sighs—every sound was a quiet alarm. I was a spectator at a drama over which I had no control.

"Now on this next contraction hold down until I tell you to let up," said Jim. "It's time we got this baby out of there."

I pushed up on Lillian's back, counting for her, pleading for her to do it. "Think that baby out, see it on the other side of you. The baby *is* moving, *is* coming. Easy, easy."

Lillian's body went rigid for the length of the contraction, and then she fell back, spent. She licked her dry lips and asked for water.

DADDY'S HOME

"Again," said Jim.

I kept a hand on her forehead, and an eye on the mirror. With a huge hypodermic needle, the student doctor jabbed a local anesthetic into her skin all around the raw opening the baby was now poised to come through.

In stages, through long minute after minute of push and shove, the baby's head slid out into the light.

"One more." Jim handed the forceps to a nurse and cradled the child's head in his hands. "Coming out now. Turn the lights down."

Again Lillian pushed, and then collapsed backward in my arms. The lights dimmed, and Lillian gasped out a loud moan.

"A girl," said Jim, evenly, without emotion. "We've got a girl here. Looks good, looks good."

"A girl!" I repeated excitedly, compensating for the doctor's professional detachment. "Lil, we've got a girl!"

Jim held the baby up, tilting her, moving her legs. He put her down on the table and prodded, checking her parts, seeing that she sucked air. He put a rubber suction bulb in her throat and squeezed, drawing from her a sharp, thin squeal.

Was that it? Was that the lusty cry of a healthy newborn? "Is she all right?"

"She's fine," said Jim.

"Ten-oh-six," said the nurse. "That was the time. Ten-oh-six. You got that?"

"Got it," said the other nurse, writing on a clipboard.

"I'd say about seven pounds," Jim mused aloud. "Come here, dad."

I took two steps to the end of the table and looked closely at my daughter. Her face was red and pinched; she looked battered. Streaks of blood and cream-white paste were smeared in patches over her body. She squirmed in annoy-

A Gently Terrific Birth

ance, lifted her arms, stretched her legs, and started in on a breathy murmur that soon became a reassuring squall of protest.

"You want to cut the cord?"

Jim handed me a pair of scissors and indicated a spot between two clamps. But I couldn't seem to get the blades on it. I was crying; my glasses had fogged. I couldn't see.

"Here, right here," said Jim, guiding my hand. I closed down on the cord. She was on her own.

As the nurses wiped her body, Jim listened to her heart, checked her reflexes. After wiping my glasses on the hospital gown, I counted fingers and toes. The count was right.

"She's in good shape, isn't she?" I said, asking for more confirmation.

"She looks fine," said Jim, smiling. "You want to hold her?"

As though she were Ming porcelain, I brought the baby to my chest and bent my face to hers. I wanted to say something special to commemorate our first meeting. But I couldn't think of anything to say. "Hey," I finally whispered. "Hey, hey. Hi, little girl."

The anxiety and tension were gone. Where minutes earlier I had worried that this child's birth might kill us all, I could think of nothing but the power of life. She was supergirl, and we were all heroic.

I imagined that we were imprinting each other. I looked into her face, fixing her indelibly in my mind while she gauged the feel of the man's hands that over the next two years would hold her more than any others. In the dim light and sterile stillness of the hospital delivery room, we acquired a primordial stake in each other. We were linked, not just by blood but by fire. I had been there when she first drew breath, and never again would I be able to think of myself without thinking of myself as this child's father.

DADDY'S HOME

A nurse took the baby from my arms and laid her on Lillian's breast. Jim and the student waited for the placenta to trail out, and then began stitching Lillian back together again.

I pulled the stool over and sat down beside Lillian, watching as the baby, now swaddled in white, rooted molelike on her chest.

"We finally did it. We did it."

Lillian squeezed my hand weakly, and smiled like the winner of a marathon. "Of course we did."

With my mind bouncing from numbness to exhilaration, I felt restless. I thought I should do something, but I did not know what to do. One minute I wanted to lie down on the floor and sleep; the next instant I had an urge to leap up whooping, and celebrate like Zorba the Greek. I wanted to embrace Jim and thump him on the back, kiss the nurses, and propel Lillian up off the delivery table into a mad tarantella.

But I didn't do anything. I sat dumbly, childstruck, staring fixedly at the girl who had made us parents. She looked so small, so vulnerable. Until that moment, the idea that I was to be a househusband, and for at least the next two years devote my time and attention to caring for a baby, had only been that—an idea. We could see evidence of the baby growing, feel it kicking, but it had had no face, no gender, no room to yell and squirm and claim a space in my concept of the world.

Now, watching her wriggle on Lillian's breast, I realized that this child would never stray outside the range of my consciousness. She was as much a part of me as my arm.

The smiling nurse picked up the baby, saying that she would be taken to the nursery. When Lillian had been sewn together, the other nurse wheeled her to the maternity ward while Jim led me to the room crowded with newborns.

A Gently Terrific Birth

Our baby was already sleeping, comalike. Jim unwrapped the pink blanket and ran his hands over the length of her, looking for defects, feeling for problems.

"She seems in excellent shape. Good heartbeat, no signs that the birth put her in damaging stress. Looks like you've got a fine little girl."

"I can't believe it. I didn't think she was ever coming out."

"It was tough. Lil hung in there."

"Yeah," I agreed, again marveling at Lillian's strength. "I was the one about to drop out."

"You did fine. You were a good coach." Jim put a hand on my shoulder. "It's hard to watch from the bench when you're used to playing, isn't it?"

I nodded tiredly.

"But now you get into the game. Some fathers never do."

By 11:30 P.M., Lillian was ready to sleep. I kissed her goodnight and walked outside into a fresh breeze that rustled the corn in fields that ran right up to the hospital parking lot. I slumped into the car and sat motionless, my hands on the steering wheel, wondering whom I could talk to. I was wound up and needed to tell my story.

Without having decided where I was going, I started the car and began to drive the eight blocks toward home. When I passed the Donovans' house, I remembered Ed's wrench was still in the trunk. A light was on.

"Mike," said Ed, a disheveled, friendly man who operated the college's computers. He was a master mechanic, and had recently helped us put new brakes on the Volkswagen. "What's up?"

"I brought back your wrench."

"Hey, fine."

"And also," I said, unable to maintain the pretense any further than that, "I just had a baby."

85

DADDY'S HOME

"You did! Wonderful! How's Lillian? The baby? Come in!"

For two hours Ed, his wife, Rita, and I drank beer and talked about birth, children, and being parents. They had two sons, both teen-agers. They remembered. They let me run on until empty.

"We were timing contractions for about twenty-four hours," I said. "I can't believe it's over."

"Over?" said Rita. "It's just beginning."

"You mean the easy part's over," said Ed.

"Well, I guess I mean that the part where you worry about something going wrong is over."

"No. That's not over either," said Rita. "That part only gets worse."

"Worse?"

"It's always there. It's being a parent."

I looked at Rita. She was a large woman with warm hazel eyes. She reminded me of somebody's mother from my childhood. I felt comfortable with her. She was thinking of something, hesitating to speak.

"What?" I prodded.

"Oh, I was just thinking. . . . Jimmy was almost two months premature, in an incubator for six weeks. He was a twin. We lost his brother."

"Oh," I said.

"I'm sorry. I didn't bring that up to get morbid. It's just that I remember how hard it was not to be able to hold him."

"Now Jimmy's thirteen, and again we can't hold him," said Ed. He walked back in from the kitchen with two cans of beer and set one on the table beside me. "One more. Then you'd better get some sleep. You start work tomorrow, don't you?"

Work? Yes, of course. Tomorrow I start work as a father.

A Gently Terrific Birth

"I guess I do."

"Lillian is not coming home tomorrow, is she?" Rita asked.

"No. In a couple of days."

"Well, take advantage of the help in the hospital."

"Are you ready for your new job?" Ed grinned.

"Can you be ready?"

"No," laughed Rita. "You can just be rested."

I went home and made telephone calls until 3:00 A.M. I roused my parents, my brother, my sister, Lillian's sister, and, when I got a second wind, a friend from the journalism program whom I had not talked to in six months.

I went to sleep feeling strangely alone. I had a family, and I missed them.

Chapter 7

Our Child, Our Responsibility

IN A BLEARY TRADITION, I awoke to my first full day as a father with a hangover. My eyes burned, my head pulsed in a dull throb, and, when I made my way to the bathroom, my body pleaded to return to bed.

It was almost noon. If I did not show up at the hospital soon, Lillian would wonder where I was. Fortunately, I thought, I would not have to do much actual childcaring on my first day of fatherhood. The hospital staff would look after Lillian and the baby. I could concentrate on getting some rest.

Driving past the Community Center I noticed two young women chatting amiably as they pushed baby strollers down the sidewalk. In the golden brightness of the late-summer

Our Child, Our Responsibility

sun, they seemed part of a timeless tableau of American life: mothers and children in unhurried communion.

Ahead, my own child, and her mother, waited. I imagined Lillian in bed, the baby in her arms. I had known Lillian as student and professional woman and companion and lover, but her new identity as a mother seemed foreign, so striking in its unfamiliarity.

And our baby: Who was she? What would she turn out to be like? What kind of bond would grow between us? What difference would it make to her that for the next two years I would be the one to settle her in her stroller and push her down the street on an afternoon walk?

Lillian was sitting up in bed, reading. She looked surprisingly chipper.

"You must be feeling pretty good."

"I feel like I've lost seven and a half pounds of live weight and a ton of energy. And I'm sore. But other than that . . ."

"Where's the kid?"

"She'll be back in a few minutes for a feeding. We had one attempt at the breast this morning." She indicated with a raised eyebrow that the attempt had gone badly.

"No good, huh?"

"We had a bad connection. But what happened to *you* last night? Your eyes are positively magenta."

"I returned Ed's wrench on the way home and stayed to describe in detail how we'd spent the day. I'll be fine as soon as I have some oxygen for breakfast."

A silver-haired nurse briskly walked in with the baby. "This must be daddy," she said jauntily. "Congratulations. You've got yourself a little doll here."

"Thank you," I said, happy to interpret her comment as more evidence that the child was healthy.

DADDY'S HOME

She put the baby on the end of the bed and lifted her out of a thin, pink blanket before handing her over to Lillian. "She should be hungry," the nurse told her. "She's had a little water this morning, but that's it. And she's been crying the hunger cry."

"The hunger cry?" I said quizzically.

"Hunger, pain, anger, frustration—they're all different. You'll get to know them."

While I silently wondered at my ignorance, Lillian untied her nightgown and cradled the baby to her breast. The round mouth closed on the nipple; but even before beginning to suck, she impatiently pulled away, complaining.

"Hold her this way, a little more parallel to the floor," directed the nurse, lifting the child's feet. "You've got to experiment until you find a position that works."

Lillian sat up straighter, and I wedged a pillow beneath her elbow.

"It's frustrating at first, but you'll get it," our nurse assured us. "You'll both get it. She's a doll."

The nurse hurried from the room, saying she would be back in a few minutes. I sat on the edge of the bed and examined our daughter, now fourteen hours old.

"You think this kid's a doll?" I asked Lillian. "She looks like a boxer who leads with her face."

She did not look like any doll I had ever seen. Her eyes had a faraway glassy cast, which made her appear uninterested, oblivious to the attention she attracted. Her complexion was blotchy, her skin wrinkled and flaking. Two large red forceps marks, like strawberry Rorschach prints, spread along the sides of her head. A downy fuzz covered her cheeks. On the back of her head was a fine, darker hair that, toward her crown, gave way to a five o'clock shadow.

She suddenly began to yell, scrunching up her face as if in pain. Then abruptly she quieted into apparent contentment. I scrutinized her in wonder; she was fascinating, an

Our Child, Our Responsibility

irresistible allure. She was brand-new, yet in her face I could see age and wisdom, the curious young-old expressions of children in Brueghel paintings. Did our child really look different from any other child I had ever seen? Or, as I studied her, looking for traces of me, had I never looked closely at a baby before?

"All girls are dolls," said Lillian. "Just like all girls get swaddled in pink. If she had been a boy, she would have been wrapped in blue and called a bruiser."

"We never talked about that, did we? That it might make a difference whether the kid I take care of was a girl or a boy?"

"Do you think it will make a difference?" Lillian seemed surprised that I would even wonder about that.

"No, I just thought of it. I'm still going to buy her a football this afternoon."

I didn't really buy her a football—not that afternoon. But I did wonder again about the difference her gender would make. Despite my intent to be an equal-opportunity father, it *would* make a difference. She would be treated like a girl, different from boys. Right away, she spared us the decision of circumcision. And right after that, her gender meant that the hospital staff put her in a pink rather than a blue blanket. On the end of her bassinet in the nursery she was identified as "Buchanan infant" by a card trimmed in pink that redundantly proclaimed, "It's a girl!"

Later, life would be different for her because she was a girl, of course. Would I dare encourage or permit her to do the things I did at ten, at fourteen, at eighteen? Could she stay out after dark, get up before dawn to deliver newspapers, hitchhike? As a girl, she was born vulnerable. Already, just hours into fatherhood, I felt protective of my daughter and angry with a world where that protectiveness seemed so appropriate.

Through the day the reminders were frequent, some more

DADDY'S HOME

subtle than others. But the message was the same: Your child was born female, and female is different. Maybe even less.

As Lillian finished her lunch, our cheery nurse came in and told us the baby would have to be returned to the nursery during general visiting hours. "And where's your gown?" she asked me.

"My gown?"

"Here," she said, grabbing a yellow smock from the empty bed next to Lillian's. "All fathers have to wear these when handling the babies."

"Color coding," said Lillian when the nurse left with our child. "Helps us remember who you are."

"Well, maybe I need something like an ID tag on my first day. But I'm not going to wear this at home."

A few minutes later, with my distinctive raiment flapping at my knees, I walked down the hallway to the large window that separated the newborns from the visitors. A woman in a floral-print dress was pointing out a child to a man in a baseball cap.

"There. She moved. See? That one with all the black hair."

"That one?"

"Yeah, that fuzzy little one. Isn't she cute?"

"You say she looks like our Mary Jo?"

"Well, she's got Mary Jo's nose, thank God, and not Junior's beak. She'll be a pretty child," she said confidently.

A low, double-rung barrier a foot and a half from the glass served to cut down on fingerprints while providing a footrest for spectators. I leaned in, looking at our daughter, who seemed to be trying to pick up her head.

A tall man with a sunburned face appeared beside me, propped a fancy cowboy boot on the rail, rested a forearm on his thigh, and, just as if we were out at the corral, said in a "Howdy, neighbor" voice: "You're a new daddy, looks like."

Our Child, Our Responsibility

"Sure am," I said, welcoming the chance to admit to fatherhood. "That's my daughter right over there."

"Buchanan. That the one?"

Just Buchanan? That hadn't sunk in before. My name was missing from the "It's a girl!" card on the bassinet. I decided not to try explaining that Lillian and I had different names, but did make a promise to myself to get my name on the card as soon as possible.

"That's the one," I said. "I think she's trying to hold up her head."

"This your first?"

I nodded.

"She looks like a real cutie pie. You must be right proud of her."

"I am. She's a bruiser."

He turned to look at me, startled by the unexpectedness of the word. When I smiled in acknowledgment of the jest, a grin crinkled his face.

"Hey, you had me going there for a minute. A bruiser. But I'll tell you, I've got four children and six grandchildren —this one over here in the corner is the seventh—and when they're little-bitty, there ain't a dime's worth of difference between them. But by the time they're walking and talking, they're either boys or they're girls. You know what I mean?" He winked in emphasis.

I lowered my brow, indicating that I wasn't sure what he meant.

"Boys'll be hellin' around from the git-go, into everything, full of piss and energy. I know, I've got three sons and three grandsons. This one here's a girl." He paused while he looked thoughtfully into the corner of the nursery.

"Girls, they're great to have, too. But they act different, and thank God for that."

Now I thought I knew what he meant. He meant, Too bad you didn't have a boy this time, but hang in there.

DADDY'S HOME

In the next fifteen minutes, as more visitors came to the glass, I realized that in front of the nursery I could, in time, hear the complete stereotypical songbook. According to these observers, the boys were stronger, more alert, bigger, more lively. The girls were quieter, weaker, less alert, finer-featured.

To me, the babies all looked about the same in size, alertness, and activity. The chief distinction I could see between one group and another was the color of the blankets in which they were wrapped.

I reported my sociological findings to Lillian.

"A victim of discrimination already," she said, teasing me with the truth of it.

"Yeah, I should have called that cowboy on it. 'Cute! That wrinkled little bawler isn't cute, and don't you ever say that about my daughter again.'"

"Right," said Lillian. "What kind of a father are you?"

That afternoon, as the temperature crept into the nineties, I bought a large box of cookies at the bakery and made the rounds of the offices on campus, announcing the birth and accepting congratulations. I began to appreciate for the first time the shared sense of parenthood, the mutual bond of responsibility and protective affection that parents feel for their children.

"You're a father," said Steve, a math teacher whose office was next to Lillian's. "It's a neat feeling, isn't it?"

It *was* a neat feeling. I was a father. There was about me an entirely new and major dimension. I was more than I had been the day before.

And the more cookies I passed out, the more I realized that the hospital cowboy was not the only one who thought a girl must have disappointed us. Our child's gender added another twist of peculiarity to our plans. I was offered more consolation.

Our Child, Our Responsibility

"Girls can do anything boys can do these days," a secretary in the Education Department told me. She did not add, "So don't be discouraged," but I heard it anyway. Boys, after all, are the gender of choice among most parents; and since I was going to stay home with our baby, a father-son dyad seemed an obvious preference.

Others I met on campus indicated that perhaps our experiment in role reversal was less dangerous to a girl, since she was by nature less serious than a boy. "A little girl, eh?" said Frank, a bearlike physical-education instructor with a large drooping moustache. He took a bite of cookie and brushed away the crumbs. "I remember—dolls, tea parties, then teen-age boys and nights of anxiety. Just relax and enjoy it."

I had bought far too many cookies. I returned to the hospital with the box and put it on the nurses' desk in the hallway. "Nobody buys cigars anymore," a heavyset, balding doctor jokingly lamented.

Our baby was sleeping in Lillian's arms. On the table beside her bed were two bunches of flowers, a large box, and three cards. "Look at that one," she said, motioning to one of the cards. On the front was a cherubic, cartoonish baby swimming in silky pink, and inside was a verse. "Sweet as a sugarplum," it read, "soft as a dove, a bundle from Heaven to pamper and love!"

"There'll be no pampering that kid," I said in mock fierceness. "It's going to be snakes and backyard adventure."

Looking at the girl, I wondered if she might be an adventurer. It would help, I thought, if she were. She was, after all, about to strike out into the world with a man as her primary guide, and while I figured that in itself would not make her infancy any more risky than others, it at least would be unconventional.

I could not determine her nature, but I could avoid pampering her, or handicapping her with cumbersome preconceptions. If she proved to have a natural affinity for snakes, she would not be forced to deny it. Maybe she could even teach me to be fonder of them.

"What else?"

"Flowers from the folks, cards from the office, and a blanket from the college president. Oh, and this." She handed me another card, this one an official-looking five-by-seven. The card asked for the child's name and birth date, so that her arrival could be recorded with the county and she could be added to the roster of the 3.4 million other people who would be born in the U.S. that year.

"What do you want to write in here?" Lillian, smiling an I-asked-you-first smile, indicated the name line.

"What did we decide?"

"We didn't."

"Maybe the kid came with a name, like T. S. Eliot's cats."

" 'Such as Bombalurina, or else Jellylorum'?" quoted Lillian.

We had discussed a host of names in the last months of pregnancy. We had consulted books designed for undecided new parents, the telephone directory, and our genealogy charts. Lillian had even made two lists of candidates, one for boys and one for girls, all of them distinctly male or female. Thus, even before birth, *we* had indicated that sex did make some difference. Sexist impediments like Butch or Dolly were out, but we would not try to conceal our child's gender in her name; that would be announced right along with identity.

Picking a name was further complicated by our own surnames. Since we each had a different last name, we agreed that our daughter should carry both of them, joined by a hyphen. But neither of us was sure in which order the names should be.

We finally decided that my name would come last in the

Our Child, Our Responsibility

compound, simply as a safeguard against confusion when she signed up for school or was drafted. If the first part of her name was misread as a middle name, or her hyphenated name became a burden, she could treat Buchanan as a middle name.

But we still hadn't decided on a first name.

"The nurse told me we can't leave the hospital with the baby until we fill out and sign these cards," said Lillian.

"Are you ready to leave today?"

"No, but let's decide this."

"Okay, what's at the top of the girls' list? Nancy, right, after both of our mothers."

"But we don't want to call her that."

"No. Let's just name her Nancy, and call her anything we like. That will take care of the tribute, and give her another option on a name later on. What do you want to call her?"

"We liked Annie."

I mulled it over, repeating the name aloud. It sounded spirited.

"Good. Then how about Kathleen for a middle name, in recognition of Irish ancestry?"

"Nancy Kathleen Buchanan-Clary. Called Annie. It's a mouthful."

I filled out the card and signed it. "Okay, what else do we need to do?"

"We need to learn all we can before we leave this place the day after tomorrow. Here, take Annie while I find something I want to read you."

Lillian slid our sleeping daughter into my arms. She wore a white hospital-issue sack and was bundled like a papoose into a double layer of pink blanket. She pursed her lips, and I could see her eyes move under paper-thin lids. The whole package felt feathery.

Lillian pulled a white booklet from a plastic bag. On the

cover were the words "Congratulations on your new baby!" Lillian read: " 'Many fathers enjoy holding babies and even feeding them—so encourage him to hold the baby during feedings. This will benefit father and child and occasionally allow you some needed free time.'

"What do you think of that?" she said.

"What's it from?"

"A baby-products manufacturer."

"Sounds like they don't have us in mind."

Why should they? Fathers were not expected to do much more than occasionally give mothers a break. But I needed to know more than how to hold and even feed our child. I needed to know everything. I needed to know how to pin a tight diaper, how to steer limp or flailing arms into pencil-size sleeves of a nightgown, how to mop up a messy bottom, and how to move a baby from one place to another while preventing her oversize head from snapping her slender neck.

I looked into Annie's face, now perfectly serene. I was not afraid of dropping her, but I was unaccustomed to her heft and balance. Several weeks earlier a friend had handed me his small son, suggesting I get in some practice. I remembered rocking the infant and directing strange noises at him, but I hadn't been comfortable; I'd had the feeling I was cradling a bomb that at any second might go off without warning. After a few minutes, with the baby wearing the same contented look he had when he came my way, I was happy to pass the child back to his father and consider my trial run a success.

Practice now was in earnest. I wanted to hold Annie, and each minute she remained in my arms I grew more comfortable. But I still had little idea about the child's daily servicing and maintenance. I needed to know that, too.

Lillian would not be able to teach me. Although as a girl, subject to the usual socialization of feminine concerns, she

Our Child, Our Responsibility

might have picked up some insights into childcare, she had no more on-the-job experience with children than I had. Like me, she might have changed the diaper of a niece or nephew once or twice under emergency conditions, but twice was a generous estimate. She was certainly more familiar with Jean Piaget's theories on the development of cognitive learning in children than she was with the proper way to give a newborn baby a sponge bath.

As a boy, and a product of a typical American boyhood, I had actually been discouraged from learning about babies and their daily care, as if too much exposure to women's work might induce me one day to forsake the man's world and do something bizarre, like stay home and care for a child.

I decided that if I required a crash course in infantcare, the hospital maternity ward seemed the place to get it. That evening, I began to seek instruction.

"Excuse me, Mrs. Palmer, but I wondered if you could give me some advice here."

Annie was on her back, kicking and screaming, her mouth wide, her tonsils in view, her dander up. I was amazed at the ferocity of her displeasure, and I was sweating in frustration. The nurse was a florid, motherly-looking woman who had first appeared with the afternoon shift. She seemed like an ideal mentor, a woman who probably had half a dozen kids of her own. If she couldn't offer some hard advice, I thought I would ask her for a sedative.

"What's the problem here, sweetie?" she inquired solicitously of Annie. "Is daddy having some trouble here?"

"Daddy is having some trouble keeping this diaper from hanging at half-mast," I said, trying to sound calm. "I'm afraid I'm going to stick a pin in her leg, or just start screaming myself."

"Here, two fingers in here, on the side, and then pull this

corner up firmly," said the nurse. She had the rectangle of cloth refolded and pulled around in seconds. "You keep your fingers here, and then if you stick anything, it will be you before the baby."

"That sounds fair."

I jumped in to pin the other side while she was still there to offer guidance. "This up here, fingers in here, and pull firmly, right?"

I did exactly what Mrs. Palmer had done, but, once pinned, the diaper still hung like an untrimmed sail.

"Almost," she said, taking over. "Pull this further around toward the back."

Annie kept up a frantic holler that had turned her face scarlet. Mrs. Palmer rewrapped the receiving blanket and picked her up.

"There, there, little girl; let's settle down," she said, patting her on the back.

"I guess I need a little practice," I said, annoyed that one of the simple chores of childcare had caused me such aggravation.

"So you're going to help mom out when you get home, are you?"

"I'm going to help mom out with the whole thing," I said with studied casualness. "I'm going to stay home with this girl while mom goes back to work."

"Well," said Mrs. Palmer, raising an eyebrow, "that's something. You do have a few things to learn then."

By the next afternoon, when word of my plans had spread through the nursing corps of the maternity wing, I was a marked man. Although one or two members of the staff seemed to write me off as one-half of an odd couple best ignored, most seemed to adopt me like a hardship case. They made me their project. I felt like Eliza Doolittle, a primitive whom a band of bemused experimenters were going to turn

Our Child, Our Responsibility

into a polished sophisticate, if not for life, at least for one sit-down dinner party.

With instruction, I learned to diaper, to tightly tuck the receiving blanket, to support her head at all times. I learned how to treat diaper rash, cradle cap, and the stump of her umbilical cord. I quickly gained confidence.

Lillian learned what I learned, along with the secrets of breast-feeding. By the time her colostrum gave way to milk, Annie was hooking up to the nipple with an unerring sense of direction. She would suck for several seconds, then swivel her head as if to survey her domain, and then return, right on target.

As Lillian finished her chicken pot pie on the evening before our departure, Jim stopped by. He had just checked Annie over in the nursery.

"She's got a touch of jaundice. Nothing serious, but she is dehydrated and needs more fluids."

"She's nursing well," said Lillian.

"Good. But she needs some water, too. I've told the nurses to get a few ounces into her."

"All right to go home tomorrow?" Lillian asked.

"If you feel up to it. What about dad?"

"Sure. I'm ready. The nurses have taught me everything."

"What do they know about being a father?" A faint smile developed in Jim's eyes.

"Father? Who needs that? I'm learning how to be a mother."

"Oh, yeah. That *would* make more sense."

That night I stayed late. I did not want to go home to sleep alone. At 10:30, Lillian nursed Annie to sleep, and then said she wanted to walk in the corridor for exercise. I took Annie and crawled into Lillian's place in bed.

DADDY'S HOME

Within what seemed like minutes, a woman in white was shaking me awake. "Sir, are you the father?"

"Yes, the father," I said to the nurse, trying to smile through my sleepiness. Annie remained quiet in my arms.

"And where is the mother?"

"I don't know."

The nurse considered us for a moment, evidently concerned about the irregularity of my behavior, but unsure whether it constituted an offense. She frowned. "You could at least have taken your boots off," she said, and then turned and walked out.

She was right. I could have taken my boots off. I had stretched out on the bed intending that my feet remain dangling over the edge. That they had managed to creep onto the covers I took only as a sign that my enthusiasm for parenthood ran high.

Seeing that my feet were again sticking into the void, I closed my eyes and prepared to return to sleep. Couvade, I thought; I was engaging in a variation of couvade. If the nurse couldn't understand it, perhaps an anthropologist could. Before Annie's birth I had gained no weight, lost none of my appetite, nor been bothered with morning sickness. I had felt no physical pains in the delivery room that could not be explained by simple fatigue. Now, however, with postpartum womb envy surfacing like bubbles, I staked my claim to a fair share of the credit and the responsibility for this child. Now that it mattered, I declared myself a father. Now, I thought, we would find out if a man could mother, too.

Chapter 8

The Inverted Macho of the Househusband

BY LATE DECEMBER a deep snowfall had cloaked the town in an alabaster wrap. On clear nights the sky was ablaze with icy stars. Stepping out on the front porch at 10:00 P.M. to let Katydog out, I inhaled strong drafts of cold air that purged my lungs, cleared my head, and filled me with a renewed sense of well-being. I went to bed refreshed, and, with Annie sleeping through most nights without interruption, I usually awoke, if not refreshed, at least more even-tempered and willing to get out of bed than at any time since her birth. Annie's new habits, her tentative recognition of night and day, her unwitting cooperation with our preferences for activity and rest, made all the difference. I was amazed, frankly, at just how trouble-free, even easy, life with a four-month-old baby had come to be. Surely, I thought, we were in the golden age of parenthood.

"Well, no wonder," I said one evening to Lillian as we sat in the living room after putting Annie down for the night. I was again rummaging through *The First Three Years of Life* by Burton L. White. "This joker says our kid's in the prime of life right now."

"Perhaps we should go to California and show her off before she starts to deteriorate," said Lillian, peering over her book.

"It's true," I said. "White says that infants her age are doers, socializers. She is a, quote, 'bon vivant in the sense of seeming to get more out of life than human beings do at just about any other time.'"

"That's pretty depressing stuff," said Lillian. "I'm not sure we should tell her it's all downhill from here."

"No, we'll withhold that," I agreed. "But seriously, how could this be the high point of her life? I remember falling in love at fourteen as downright euphoric. To say nothing of falling in love with you. But I can't recall four months at all."

"Just so she doesn't start to recall colic," said Lillian. "We're all bon vivants after that."

I shook my head, remembering. Anything beat colic. By comparison with a few weeks ago, before her bouts with colic mysteriously stopped, Annie was now a regularly scheduled angel, in her bed and usually asleep by nine o'clock, rarely stirring before 6:30 or 7:00 in the morning. During the day she played in her crib, babbled to herself while lying on the floor, conversed animatedly with Katydog in Urdu, or drew grin after grin from her doting dad, who hung over her, touching her nose or telling her impromptu stories of snowbound adventure.

The Inverted Macho of the Househusband

Books on child development, like White's and others, were useful guides, not only in suggesting what to watch for as the baby grew, but in confirming that our child was on schedule, bordering on genius. Socially and physically, she seemed to be following the textbook, unimpeded by being in the care of a man. She could grasp with coordinated, smooth movements; she enjoyed looking in a mirror; she worked diligently on turning over, on improving her strength and body control.

Our girl was a smiler, either a genuinely happy child or a schemer who had learned to control her parents like Pavlovian dogs by simply turning up the corners of her mouth to reveal her gums. By the time we were sure that she was indeed smiling, and not merely appearing to smile in response to stomach gas, we were hooked, addicted to her expressions of joy, and we were willing to reach for almost any antic heights, or stoop to any burlesque lows, to win a fix of muted hilarity.

Annie ate nothing but breast milk, and she ate regularly and with gusto. During the workday, Lillian nursed Annie in the morning before work, at home during lunchtime, once in midafternoon—after a quick dash home from her office or after we dashed there—and again at 5:00 P.M. The only times Lillian had missed a feeding were when she couldn't get away in the afternoon, or went out of town on business—and then she hand-expressed milk for storage in the freezer and I thawed it out at mealtime.

Breast-feeding, along with Annie's age and good nature, made her a natural traveler. We did not have to worry about carrying formula or packing other special foods for her; if Lillian was there, so was lunch. Nor did we worry about pacifying her in times of fretfulness; she was always willing to nurse, at least briefly. And we knew she was eating as well as was possible.

We decided to fly to California. We wanted Lillian's

DADDY'S HOME

parents to meet our amiable baby at the magical age between colic and independent mobility; furthermore, I wanted to show off what I had learned. If I had not exactly demystified motherhood, I at least was confident that I could make an impressive case for father. I had not been merely baby-sitting for the last four months. I had mastered a few tricks of the childcare trade, and I was ready to go on the road.

Walking toward a distant departure gate in the Detroit airport, I was struck by the idea of family. For the first time since Annie's birth, I was aware of the three of us as a unit, a unique partnership, publicly visible and somehow distinguished among the scurrying throng of rushing, preoccupied people. I was, for me, dressed up, way up. Not only did I have on a long-sleeved shirt—the kind I used to wear to work—but I wore a belt with my clean corduroy Levi's. Lillian, in slacks and hooded jacket, carried a suitcase and the diaper bag. I had the other suitcase and Annie, who was agape at the commotion around her.

Ticketed and checked in, we sat in the lounge and waited, mother, father and baby, much like a number of other families of three I had noticed in the airport. Many young children, echoes of the miniboom in babies, were apparently being shuttled off to meet grandparents during the holidays. But with Annie happily idling on my knee, I thought again how different we were from the others, and I imagined that difference was noticeable to the close observer: the proprietary expression in my eyes, the practiced way I held our child, Annie's total trust and familiarity with my touch. Could any of these other new fathers match this facile know-how?

Sitting quietly, thankfully composed, I imagined projecting a silent swagger, an inverted macho, a reverse chic, that said to all around us: "Hey! Can you imagine being so masculine as to risk being responsible for childcare and

The Inverted Macho of the Househusband

housekeeping and domestic concerns?" I was engagingly blasé, coolly nonchalant, but in full control, the way blond teen-age surfers always seemed to be on the breakers of California or Australia. How do they *do* that! I often marveled to myself on the beach, and there in the airport I thought I could hear the same refrain from the passing crowd.

I was prepared to handle emergencies on the plane. Should Annie be alarmed by the roar of takeoff, I would comfort her. Should she need changing during the flight, I would change her. Should she begin to fuss and demand attention, I would walk her down the aisle, soothing her with practiced expertise while our fellow passengers watched in wonder. As we took our seats, I was a nerveless oil-well fire fighter, ready for a wildcat eruption.

But the trip was uneventful. Lillian nursed Annie during lift-off and landing, and I was given no cause to make a show of my talents or job classification. There were no crises, no alarms, no fires. Even the flight attendants, who from the start treated Annie like a highly sensitive bomb that posed a constant threat, seemed surprised by her pacific nature.

"She's so good," raved one young stewardess, bringing us another handful of saltines.

"What are we supposed to be doing with all these crackers?" I asked Lillian in puzzlement.

"I think it's just part of their training," she answered. "They see a baby and they grab for the crackers, no matter what the child's age."

In California the Christmas rain had turned the foothills green and made mud of the tawny clay paths between citrus trees. Driving from the airport to Lillian's parents' home in the orange grove, we retraced the route we had taken just a year before after learning that we would have a child. I remembered my reckless exuberance over the news. Today

DADDY'S HOME

the ditches ran with rainwater. Doves still hunched on the wires. But somehow, heading south through the valley under lowering clouds, my child asleep in the back seat of the rented car, I felt more than just a year older, more sober. The feeling was uncomfortable. Perhaps I was making too much of my role, perhaps I was taking my job too seriously, exaggerating the demands of being a full-time father as compensation for the loss of my professional status.

Lillian, sitting next to me in the front seat, stared straight ahead. Her thick brown hair hung down in a fringe around her narrow, angular face. She looked tired.

As we pulled onto the dirt road leading to the house, Lillian's parents were outside waiting. They exulted over Annie, their third grandchild, their first granddaughter.

"I think she looks like you," Lillian's mother said to me.

I was pleased. "It's probably all the time we spend together," I said smiling.

"And how is all that time going?" asked Bill.

"It's going fine," I replied with conviction. "I'm like an astronomer discovering a new galaxy. She's a great kid, a new world. But really," I confided, "the work is not that hard."

Throughout the four-day visit, I was on vacation. Not only did Nancy gladly help care for Annie, but Lillian, away from the college for the first time since the baby's birth, assumed more than a half-share of the responsibility for her. I willingly relinquished my claim to equal time. Although I wanted to impress Lillian's parents with my facility for childcare, I did not feel obliged to appear tireless, to play earth father. I relished the chance to engage in strenuous, more traditionally masculine pursuits. When not helping Bill cut firewood, or clear brush from the grove, I walked with the dogs to the tops of the foothills, following the flight of red-tailed hawks riding the updrafts, or stalked jackrabbits with a camera and a telephoto lens.

The Inverted Macho of the Househusband

In the late afternoon, as rainwater trickled through the downspouts, I stretched out on the bed in the back bedroom and, in letters, tried to get a bearing on just where, on the shifting sea of fatherhood, I was.

When people ask me how I am faring as a househusband, I invariably answer, "Fine." And that seems to be true. When I mentally list the problems and disappointments of the first four months, the first thing I think of is Katydog's acute case of jealousy. At first she was curious about Annie. Every time I sat down, with or without the baby, the dog would run over and jam her snout into my hand, double-time her tail, and cry, "Pet me!" And although she has backed off some, she's still upset. After six years as an only child, this stranger comes along and demotes her to family pet. I anticipate a mitigating development soon: solid food. In a few months, when we put Annie in a high chair and begin to feed her things like bananas and pepperoni pizza, I expect the dog will learn that a kid can be pretty provident, slinging food every which-a-way. Katydog will hang under her chair like a grateful beggar, and forget her hurt.

Here in California I became aware of something else. Away from home and our routines, we seem prone to fall into a pattern of traditional male and female roles. Lil spends more time caring for Annie than I do, perhaps out of guilt from being away so much, or perhaps because I simply let her, or perhaps because her parents encourage the pattern. And of course, I would rather be out bird-watching or confronting a stubborn stump than mopping up Annie or dealing with her fussiness. I also like getting dirty. What does that say about my socialization or my genes?

There is also the question of crying: How much is enough? At bedtime we let her run, and sleep overtakes her in short order. But during the day, when she demands attention, the controversy quietly rages. It's tough for grandparents, who know exactly what to do, but who won't tell out of fear of interfering. Here, when Annie is inconsolable, I look out the window and always seem to sight a rare warbler that demands tracking. And I run outside. What's a vacation for if not escape?

DADDY'S HOME

The trip home was almost without incident. The only spot of trouble I brought on myself. After Annie began insisting on a diaper change, I insisted on taking her to the lavatory to perform it. I don't know why. But once in there, crammed in close to the loudly droning jets, I made a mess of her and me. I was the sticky-fingered essence of the bungling father stereotype, out of his league with an infant in distress. Then, to make a bad scene worse, the plane began to shake, and a red light over the sink began to flash, urgently ordering me back to my seat. I was sure that the plane was about to flame out over the Rocky Mountains. I found no comfort in knowing that I *always* think the plane is going to flame out whenever I am sitting on the john at thirty-five thousand feet.

I rushed the cleanup, further maddening Annie, and hurried back to my seat. She was screaming furiously, and virtually naked. And I had been exposed. We fell into the seat beside Lillian, who for a minute seemed inclined not to recognize us. Eventually she clamped Annie to her breast, and the baby's turbulence subsided as the seat-belt sign went off.

"Had the plane started to rumble to pieces before we went to the bathroom, or did we set that off?" I asked her.

"I'm not sure which came first," said Lillian in mock earnestness. "But people *were* looking for parachutes."

We all were relieved to be home, to settle in for the winter. Over the next few weeks I got all the storm windows up, and painted the basement darkroom. Annie learned to arch her back, and eventually turned over unassisted. She ate banana and liked it. We seemed to be thriving. But still I wondered: What should I be doing, what was it I missed?

Chapter 9

The Only Man in the Park

USUALLY, I was the only man in the park. While Annie swung with the other children, I stood and pushed with the mothers. Over the years adult hands had worn away the blue paint on the backs of the bucket seats. Grassless grooves in the earth showed me where to stand. The footholes were slightly too close together for me, but, just as I did when I faced left-handed pitching, I adjusted my stance.

We became known as weekday-afternoon regulars.

"Annie looks cute in that jumper. Is it new?" Frances was in her accustomed seat at the picnic table, watching her two children in the sandbox. She always had an open book in her hands, but I don't think she ever read.

DADDY'S HOME

"Yes, I just got it from Christine next door. Her boy's outgrown it."

"Looks good on her," said Frances. "And what a day, eh?"

"Perfect."

It was a Tuesday in early July, one of those days when there is no top to the sky and the cool air from thirty thousand feet settles like a protective dome over the town as if to preserve in freshness an idealized midwestern scene. The day was air-conditioned, sunny, very green. Periodically, the voice of a child would break through the crispness like a bell.

We had been coming to the park almost daily for more than a month, since the icy spring relented. The park was important to Annie and me. After the long winter of our infancy, we both needed the people, the activity, and the socializing we found there. We also needed a destination, and the park gave us a handy one.

By the time the cicadas began filling the afternoon with their treetop droning, the park had become a constitutional in which we honed our identities—hers as a child of ten months, mine as a housespouse, maturing with experience.

Annie had immediately recognized the park as a place intended for her, filled with toys and activity and other people her size. In the park, with her nose inches from another small nose, I imagined her having her first Hegelian insight, confirming her existence in the acknowledgment of others. In the park, I could see my daughter becoming herself.

For me the park provided reassurance. I met other adults there, doing what I was doing, minding their children with the same casual watchfulness that never let them stray out of the corner of the eye. In the children's vitality and appearance, we publicly measured our performance as parents. We

The Only Man in the Park

offered them up as proof of what we did, and how well we did it.

My peers were women, and if there was an initial strangeness to my difference, it soon passed. Usually it was just the mothers, the children, and me. So when another man showed up that gentle Tuesday, he drew our surprised attention.

"How're ya doin'?" He smiled broadly at me as he helped a toddler with a Dutch-boy haircut into the swing next to Annie. Like me, he was wearing a T-shirt, jeans, and tennis shoes. He had curly blond hair and was, I guessed, about eight or ten years younger than I. He looked familiar, but I was sure I had not seen him in the park before.

Within seconds, Annie and the boy were staring at each other curiously as they sailed back and forth in tandem arcs. The blond man took up a position on my left, and we joined together in a rhythmic push, our fingers flexing against the cool metal of the seats. The chain in its coupling repeated a metronomic squeak that kept us on stroke.

"A new friend, Annie," I said. And to his father I added, "What is he, about two?"

"Twenty months. That's Bradley."

"This is Annie. She's just half as old."

"Hi, Annie," he said exuberantly. "Nice day, huh? Man, it's great to be out today."

"Yeah," I said, already feeling some sense of kinship between us. "These are the days that revive the spirits."

We pushed on in silence. Was it possible, I wondered, that this man could be a househusband like me? The chances seemed remote. In the preceding months I had read of other men with jobs like mine, but those men all seemed to be in Boston or Seattle. There were a few representatives of the phenomenon on each coast, I figured, and me in the middle. Certainly if there had been another househusband in our small town, I would have homed in on him long ago.

DADDY'S HOME

And yet here it was, 1:45 in the afternoon on a working day. And where had I seen this guy before?

"You look familiar. Have we met before?"

"I was thinking the same thing," he said, puzzled. "I don't know. I've seen you. . . ."

"You're not at the college?"

"No, I teach high school over in Burton."

"Tennis? You play tennis at the college courts?"

"No. But basketball—"

"Basketball. That's it. You used to play Saturdays in the gym. Yeah, we played."

"Right, right."

I remembered him now. Green jersey. Not a bad player. Fast and savvy, but he shot too much.

"Kids can swing forever, can't they? Bradley is always begging me to take him to the swings."

"Annie loves it, too. It's hypnotic."

"I tied up an old tire to a tree limb at our house, but he still wants to come to the park. And we live so far out in the country, it's a big production to get here. But it gives us something to do, and we try to combine it with trips for groceries."

He *did* stay home! He *was* a househusband! I was *not* alone!

"You home with Bradley all the time?"

"Yeah, for the summer, anyway. It's sort of an experiment. I usually work a landscaping job for three months. But my wife wanted to go back to work, so . . ." He shrugged and gave me a "no big deal" look.

"How do you like it?"

"Oh, it's not bad. Not all that exciting. I like spending time with this guy." He tousled his son's hair on the backswing.

"It's a job, isn't it?"

The Only Man in the Park

He rolled his eyes. "Amazing. I wonder sometimes how watching one twenty-month-old can be harder than trying to teach algebra to a roomful of sophomores."

"I know," I said, grinning in recognition. I was starting to feel sanguine about the potential of our fraternal bond. "I'm full-time with Annie."

"You off for the summer, too?"

"No, for a couple of years."

"Oh," he said. He turned back to face his son, a trace of a faraway look in his eyes.

Two long-haired girls about six, in shorts and T-shirts, ran toward us and jumped into the swings to the left of Bradley. He and Annie followed them intently, silently. In seconds the girls were soaring, hair flying about their faces.

"What's your wife do?" I asked.

"She's an accountant. Making good money, too."

"Have you considered quitting teaching to stay home longer?"

"We've talked about it," he said, without enthusiasm. "In fact, that's kind of what this summer is about—to find out if we like the switch." He smiled and shook his head slowly.

"But . . ."

"I don't know. I think I'd miss working. Even teaching sophomores."

"But *this* is work," I said, like it was a joke.

"Oh, sure. But it's—it's too slow. It just doesn't suit me as well as it does my wife. And besides, Bradley's getting to the age where he's going to start to wonder what I do for a living."

"He is?" I said, surprised.

I looked at Bradley. His hair had his father's color but none of its curl. Swinging beside Annie, he didn't seem close to worrying about what his father did for a living. He looked blissfully carefree.

DADDY'S HOME

"Well, you know, the role-model thing," he said.

I furrowed my brow in response, urging him to elaborate. I began to suspect that we would not be soulmates after all.

"I'm no chauvinist," he said. "I think I do my share with Brad. But I just think I need to work more than my wife does. Maybe we both need to work. But I was never geared to stay home all the time. Plus, I think it will be better for him as he gets older to see his father working."

"Hmmm," I said, noncommittal.

"It's not really critical in your case, because you have a girl."

"What!" A minute ago I had liked this guy.

"The identification is not as strong as father to son. She has your wife as a role model." He appeared flustered, and I refused to help him out by smiling.

"And you think that if you stay home too long, your son will get the idea that men don't really work, and that would be bad for him?"

"Well, it would be misleading. It's not the way the world is. But I really think *I'd* be better off working. I just don't get enough satisfaction out of staying home."

"Sounds like you think girls are somehow less important than boys."

"No, no. I didn't mean that. It's just that girls are more likely to stay home, raise children, keep house, that sort of thing. And I don't find it all that stimulating."

Bradley stuck his arm out toward Annie, indicating that the swings had fallen out of synchronization. I adjusted the rhythm.

"You have to work at it," I said. Now I was the professor, taking the inattentive student to task. "You don't get much in the way of a paycheck or job title."

He nodded in agreement. "Why do you like it?"

The Only Man in the Park

"Well..." Suddenly I wished I had more time to prepare an answer. I didn't want to deliver an essay, but at the same time, I thought, I was being invited to make a major defense of my life. In ten months, no one had ever asked me exactly that before.

"Well, like you said, you get to know your child. You get a chance to learn some things about what women do. Most men never get that chance. And you learn that working a regular job might not be so important."

"Aha!" he said, blazing through the opening I'd given him, heading for the basket. "For me, that's just it. My regular job must be more important than I thought. I don't mean you can't be a man without a job. But I need more action. That's just my nature, I guess."

The two girls leaped off the swings and raced away. In the uneasy silence that fell between us, I felt disappointed, betrayed, like I had lost a friend. What did I want? Everybody had their own reasons. He felt no more kinship with me than I with him.

He glanced at his watch. "Hey, twenty after two, Brad. Gotta go get your mother's cleaning, and then buy some groceries." He grabbed one of the chains of the swing and sent his son into a spastic twist. Bradley yelped in protest.

At least he does the grocery shopping, I said to myself. But I'll bet he doesn't do the cooking.

"Maybe we'll see you guys here again," I said.

"Yeah, good to see you," he replied, carrying Brad away. "Take care."

Strangely wounded, I bicycled us home. It was naptime. On the bed upstairs I emptied the sand from Annie's shoes and changed her diaper and shirt. I saw that she was getting a suntan on her arms.

With Annie in her crib, I retreated to the study, where

DADDY'S HOME

I sat staring at the typewriter keys. I was vaguely aware of the squabbling English sparrows and the intermittent whoosh of traffic on the street in front of the house.

In many ways, Brad's father and I were alike. We were both volunteers. We both loved our children and enjoyed being with them. We were both dependent on our wives for support.

But yet we were different. He felt naked without his job. Relying on his wife for money bothered him. I understood that. But did he know where to look for the little payoffs scattered through the days at home like sparklers in the dark?

Maybe he got started too late. Was he there for Bradley's birth? Did he get his hands wet during the first twenty months? Did Bradley's cries come through on his frequency as clearly as they did on his wife's?

I should have invited him over to the house. We could have gone into Annie's room, and I would have pointed out what to look for. Watching her sleep, we could see Annie clench and unclench her hands, see her face twitch as in a bad dream, and listen for the huge, shuddering sighs that rolled up out of her infant depths like gear changes in a Mack truck.

"Don't you ever wonder what's going on in there?" I would ask him. "Do you ever think you spend too much time just watching Bradley sleep?"

Sure, there were days when I would have traded my job at home for just about anything short of executioner. With a handful of inconsolable infant, or a toilet bowl full of diapers and diarrhea, even a spot on a fast-moving assembly line sounded attractive.

But the rewards were there, too, and I began to discover them when I gave up my attempts to control the shape of

The Only Man in the Park

the day, to make things happen, or predict what Annie would do. I learned to pay attention, to watch her closely, to enjoy her like a flower unfolding.

I was there when she discovered her big toe. She stuck it in her mouth, and it entered her consciousness. I wrote down the time in her scrapbook, and quietly rejoiced.

I gave Annie her first solid food: cold cooked carrots, lunchtime, January 4. She seemed to like them, and it amazed me. I thought they tasted terrible.

When she was just shy of six months, she learned to turn over by herself. I remember putting her down on her stomach for a nap, and when I heard her softly gurgling two hours later, she was on her back, blithely batting at toys that hung over her crib. She looked profoundly pleased with herself.

She learned to crawl, and practiced incessantly. She forced us to put the houseplants out of reach, raise the stereo, and rearrange the furniture.

Between the time she awoke at seven and the time she went down for the night, about thirteen hours later, our days were full of tiny turns and small advances that demanded I look closely. Alone, they seemed insignificant. But cumulatively, as evidence of growth, they were the rewards, available to mothers and fathers. To earn them, the parent had to be there, and put in the time.

Didn't Bradley's father read to his son? Annie and I spent hours each day with books. At first she liked to chew them, throw them, or tear the pages. But as soon as she could make out the pictures, she liked to hear them read. Books were her passion.

Some books she liked more than others, and she liked them repeated. I grew sick of some, bored with others. We read a few books so often that passages are committed to memory, I think forever.

> Said Farmer Brown, "Tra-la, tra-lee!
> Today is my birthday, lucky me!
> I'll give my animals a treat—
> for each, what he likes best to eat."

Along with her favorite books, I read aloud from some of mine—*Moby Dick,* the poems of Theodore Roethke, Pablo Neruda, and Walt Whitman:

> Behold, the body includes and is the meaning, the main concern, and includes and is the soul;
> Whoever you are, how superb and how divine is your body, or any part of it!

She taught me. She was a natural, waving her arms, kicking her legs, discovering new sounds, and exploring new positions. She surprised herself. When she intertwined her fingers over her chest, her eyes widened and she looked at me, amazed, as if unable to believe that hands could fit together so perfectly.

Lying down beside her on the bed, I relearned lessons of childhood, the lessons of Zen, the truth of the body; our muscles and joints know what to do if only the mind does not interfere. Reminded that I naturally had it in me to hit a solid backhand, I could turn Annie over to Lillian in the late afternoon and meet Roger on the tennis court, prepared to shut off the stream-of-consciousness coaching that went on in my head. And when I let my body play in peace, the ball would jump off my racket and skid low over the net like a bullet.

"Hey! Where'd you get that shot?" Roger looked stunned.

The Only Man in the Park

"Annie taught me."

"Damn. And I thought all she was teaching you was patience."

Patience was just a part of the curriculum. She taught me caution, responsibility, anguish, trust. She taught me to plan ahead. We never went anywhere without at least three extra diapers and a bottle of orange juice.

She taught me respect for the power of life. I learned to slow down. I learned to recognize the way she controlled me. I found out that if I wanted to make bread for dinner, I would have to get it mixed and punched down in the bowl before she woke up from her nap, because once awake she somehow sucked up all of my attention.

Were these lessons lost on Bradley's father? Did I exaggerate? Was I turning drudgery into sublimity in an effort to justify myself?

The doorbell started Katydog barking, and I ran downstairs to restore quiet. Roger, dressed in a blue blazer and sharply creased slacks, was sitting on his bicycle at the door.

"Hey, you want to wake the baby!" I scolded.

"Oops. You want to play tennis after work?"

"I'll call Lil and see if she's going to be home at five. But while you're here, come in a minute, will you? I need some help."

I indicated the couch in the living room. "Annie keeps crawling back there and getting stuck. I want to move it over there, up against that far wall."

"I'm not dressed for heavy labor," Roger protested.

"It's not that heavy. You won't even work up a sweat."

We walked the couch across the room, and slid it flush to the wall. "I'll get the chairs later. Thanks. Say, we were down swinging in the park a little while ago—"

"What a rough life you have," Roger interrupted.

"—and I was talking with that blond, curly-haired guy

we've played basketball with in the gym. You know him. He's a schoolteacher."

"Oh, James Kirby. What's he doing hanging around the park?"

"He's home with his son."

Roger shook his head in mock disgust. "That's what I need, a job hanging around the park. You guys have it made."

"I don't know if you could handle it," I said.

"Hell. Nothing to it. Annie sleeps half the time, right? I could run an antique-refinishing business on the side."

"Ha. Well, all you have to do is get yourself a kid and you're in business."

"That's what Susan says. Sometimes I wish I *could* stay home."

"Why not?" I said, now serious.

Roger looked at me as if the answer were obvious and he need not reply.

"In fact," I said, "you don't even need a kid. Just stay home. Susan makes enough."

"Oh, I can't drop out now, not if I'm going to get anywhere in administration," he said, as if annoyed by the very idea. "I've got seven years in this."

"But Susan's got a career, too."

"Sure. That's what I keep telling her. She can have a career or a child." He laughed, and moved for the door. "I just wish I had your schedule. What are you going to do now, take a nap?"

Roger swung his long leg over the bike seat. "Call me," he said, and rode off.

I stood in the doorway and watched him disappear behind the chapel, thinking that for the second time in less than two hours two men who seem so like me in many ways had told me they were not like me at all. Neither one was able

The Only Man in the Park

to call himself a househusband without some misgiving or regret. James Kirby had said there was nothing in it, and Roger told me there was nothing to it.

It didn't make sense. There *was* something to it. And how could Roger say he would love to be in my place, and then turn around and offer his career as an excuse for never really being able to do it? Did he want to stay home or not?

I called Lillian. "Are you going to be home at five?"

"I can be," she said.

"I have to meet Roger, man-to-man, on the tennis court. I'm going to whip his ass."

"Uh-oh. What happened?" asked Lillian.

"Nothing, really. I'm just having a rush of testosterone."

"Going macho on me, huh? Hold on; I'll be there."

Chapter 10

The Father as Son

MINUTES AFTER FIVE O'CLOCK, Katydog and I jogged over to the slab of green asphalt where so often I chased the day's accumulated frustrations by whaling a fuzzy yellow ball. The dog stalked squirrels between oak trees while Roger and I played our usual erratic game, full of great ideas, misfires, and accidental brilliance, through two hot sets. As usual, we split, one each. Katydog caught no squirrels.

Afterward, we sat on a bench toweling off in satisfying tiredness, and I felt glad that Roger and I were so evenly matched.

The Father as Son

"If you stop by the house," I told him, "I'll buy you a beer."

"Thanks, but I've got to get home. It's my night to start dinner." He inspected the strings on his racket and slipped it into the cover. "I was thinking, by the way, about what I said earlier, about staying home. Sometimes I really think I would like to do what you do. But I couldn't. Now if I was a writer like you . . ."

He stood up, slinging his towel around his neck. "I guess my job is too important. My father always said that without a job you're nothing. I guess I believed him. Your father was probably different."

"Yeah."

"Anyway, I like what I'm doing. And I'm happy that you like what you're doing."

"Sometimes it's hard to remember that what I'm doing is a job," I said, getting to my feet.

"That's the problem," said Roger. "Gotta go."

"See you tomorrow."

Katydog and I walked across campus toward home, trailing long shadows behind us. Chimney swifts, the flying cigars of the early evening, frantically whirled over the rooftops, clicking like windup toys. What oddball birds they were.

What about me? I guessed I was sort of an oddball myself. Could I lay that on my father, or my parents? Were they really so different? Seen from a demographic distance, they were average midwestern folks. They each had little more than a high-school education, they worked hard and lived comfortably as responsible citizens tending traditional, mildly conservative values and attitudes. When I and my younger brother and sister, Stephen and Patricia, were growing up, our parents had passed along to us their belief in

DADDY'S HOME

proper grammar and good manners. We were required to do our homework before going to bed. And each Sunday the five of us went to church, not so much because mom and dad were filled with Christian obligation, but because they saw church as an appropriate place for us to learn the universal ethic: Do as you would have done.

My father believed in work as a responsibility. He never told me in so many words that without a job a man was nothing, but I think he held as tightly to that opinion as did Roger's father. Certainly my dad's job was central to his identity; and when judging the success of his children, especially his sons, our jobs were critical, too. What we did was in part a measure of his success as a father, and when we gained status, he rose with us.

Dad was always generous in his expressions of pride. I remembered the way he introduced me to his friends after I had made the little-league team. I was nine years old.

"This is my boy, Mike," he said, a little too loudly, when he took me by his local tavern that Saturday afternoon in May in a suburb of Chicago. "He was the youngest one to make the Hornets today. Going to hold down right field."

"Hey, great going," said the bartender. "Ben, you must be pleased. You gave him some good coaching."

"Nah, he's a natural, Tony," said dad, directing me to a stool at the bar. "Give him a root beer."

I got encouragement and praise for getting good grades in school, for having friends, for being interested in girls and in sports, for choosing heroes like Hopalong Cassidy and baseball players.

There was a test going on, an entrance exam into manhood, and I passed without ever realizing that an examination was taking place.

Only after finishing college in the mid-1960s did I see that I had begun to displease my father. The antiwar move-

The Father as Son

ment, San Francisco, communal living, rock 'n' roll rebellion, hair down to there—he did not understand these attractions, and when I would come home for a visit an undercurrent of tension ran through the house and made everyone edgy. Confused by my behavior, dad retreated, communicated with silences. My choosing to stay home with a baby appeared to him as one more act of rash rebellion—against what, he could not imagine.

Yet, I thought, as a young man he had been a rebel himself. Had he forgotten? As one of six children born to an Irish family in a western Pennsylvania mill town, my father had seemed destined to become a blue-collar worker like most of his brothers and high-school classmates. But instead of going into the factory, he had left town.

Abashed by the poverty of his own childhood, my father's ambition as a young man was to provide for his family a more comfortable life than the one he had had as a boy. And he did. He wore a white shirt and sold everything from hardware to inventory appraisals in order to move his wife and three children into a new ranch house in the suburbs.

He changed his life, and our lives, but my father never changed a diaper. Nor, as far as I remember, did he ever cook a meal, help with the housework, or stay home with us when we were sick. We were, growing up in the 1940s and 1950s, a traditional American family: Father earned the money, and mother kept the home and children.

So where did I get the idea that I could buck tradition? If I got the confidence from dad, I got the inspiration from mom. When dad drew away, mother made up the distance. Preparing for my life as a househusband and father, it was she who took me seriously, gave me approval, passed on her recipe for no-fail strawberry pie.

My mother lived a childhood as charmed as my dad's was

rough. As a girl, ten years older than her only sibling, a brother, she was lavished with attention by her parents and a large circle of prosperous relatives in Sharon, Pennsylvania. She spent summers at home in the country, where her father was a gentleman farmer, and the school year in town with Aunt Mary, an independent, well-traveled Christian Scientist from whom she inherited a love of books, a strong faith, and a plucky determination. Mother grew up well centered, sure she was special, brimming with a mind-over-matter confidence that later, to her children, shone like serenity through her pale green eyes.

Of course mother was a superb cook, tireless housekeeper, resourceful nurse, wise adviser and counselor, chauffeur, confidante, and friend. When money was short, she went to work as a secretary or receptionist, sometimes working at night. In the age of Supermoms, she was, to the three of us, a paragon, a Wondermom. But in addition to comfort and love and care, I counted on mother as a wellspring of steadfast composure. And she was scrupulously honest. I knew, for example, when I was ten and wide-eyed with fear over impending surgery for a hernia, that if she said she would be there when I awoke, she would be. She would never lie. But I also knew that she was assuring me that I would awaken.

I learned to draw strength from that faith. Alarmed by Annie's sudden fever, or fluctuations in her appetite, I called the doctor, or referred to a book. Confused by the directions for suspending the swing seat from the doorjamb, I asked for help from Lillian or from Christine next door. But when in doubt about how to be a father to Annie, I relied on what I had learned during my childhood, a childhood that now seemed so secure, so free of trauma, so seamless. I knew I could give Annie my love but not my ideas. I could give her approval, but I could not control what she did with the

The Father as Son

self-confidence she made from that approval. I invested in the faith of my parents.

When I walked into the house, Lillian chuckled. "You must have won," she said.

"No, split as usual. Why? Do I look victorious?"

"You were smiling like Bjorn Borg accepting the check."

"Well, we are alike in many ways," I said, posing for a crushing overhead.

"You both wear shorts," Lillian teased.

"Really, I was thinking on the way home that I hope Annie likes sports."

"Will she have any choice?" Lillian said wryly.

"Sure. It will mean forfeiting her inheritance, but I suppose she doesn't *have* to play basketball. She probably *will* want to be a cheerleader."

Lillian made a face of displeasure. "We'll just keep playing ourselves, and if she likes us, she'll get the message. You're not thinking of giving up basketball yourself, are you?"

"Give up basketball!" I clapped my hand to my heart and fell back, feigning horror at the thought of it. "You joke. They'll have to cut off my sneakers."

Chapter 11

A Man's Game

EVEN IN THE SUMMER, the off-season, basketball remained the sweaty game of my dreams. If my identity as a househusband gave rise to any suspicions that I was somehow a hormone or two short of full masculinity, on the basketball court I could trample them down with a size eleven Converse All-Star and a resolute desire to win.

Back when Annie was three and a half months old, weeks away from her first Christmas, Roger had told me I would be eligible to play on the faculty-staff team in the college intramural league. "You're Lillian's husband," he said. "You can play as a spouse."

A Man's Game

The faculty-staff team was the huff-and-puff entry in a league where it was better to be beefy than graceful. The style of play was all elbows and floorburn. Some of my teammates were former varsity college players, several years past their prime, and others had never played competitive basketball at all. We were all old enough to be susceptible to visions that defy the years, potbellies, lack of wind, and sagging muscles.

"You guys are a dream team," one callow student used to tell us. "You're dreaming if you think you can win in this league."

In fact, our team did win more games than it lost, and that was important, to all of us. We tried to win, and when we did, we took it as evidence that our skills were barely diminished.

For me, the games were a weekly release. Through the housebound days of the cold winter, the contests provided a quickening anodyne to inaction, a hot ballet of thumping ball and gym-shoe squeak in which I could shuck off the careful gentleness of my job at home and run and jump into physical exhaustion. I loved to play.

The locker room before each game was filled with the easy, men-only banter that bred in the pregame tension. We were comrades preparing for battle. The topics of conversation were those my teammates had in common: students, other faculty and staff members, administration policy, and events in the classroom.

And women, of course, and sex.

"Fast Eddie, I hear you were seen at the bowling alley with the new librarian."

Eddie, a history professor who wore thick glasses and long dark hair, stood bouncing a basketball against a locker while he waited for the others to finish dressing for the game.

DADDY'S HOME

He was recently divorced. He did not look up at Robert.
"Where did you hear that?"
"I have informants. Any comment?"
"No."
"Come on, for Chrissakes. You going out with her or not?"
"What do you care?" Eddie grinned, but he looked bothered, too. "Jeez, we let you play coach and you think you have to know everything."
"Yeah, well, if you don't score about twenty tonight, I may have to impose a curfew. And bed checks."
Although much of the content and style of the humor was familiar, no different from locker-room joviality anywhere, as an outsider I was ignorant of much of what was under discussion. Without anecdotes of coworkers or office politics, I was different.

But on the court, stripped down to our shorts and sneakers and jockstraps, we all looked about the same. Running up and down between the ends of the court, we gasped for our share of the same overheated gymnasium air. Together we were drawn into the game as it unraveled, cheering our teammates' scores, moaning the misses. We took it seriously.

By the third game of the season, I felt like I had regained the feel of the game; the ball fit in my hands, my legs had stopped hurting, and I had remembered how to rest and catch my breath on offense. Perhaps I had just modified my expectations, or reshaped my memory of how I'd once played. But after the game, I felt good.

While some of the guys went immediately into the shower, sending cumulus clouds of steam rolling in over the tops of the tiled stalls, I sat on a bench and stared at my aching feet. The skin was peeling off both big toes, and my body temperature was close to that of a moderate oven.

"You were really hustling out there, man." John, by far

A Man's Game

the best player on the team, slumped down beside me. Six months earlier, at the baby shower, he had seemed painfully ill at ease. But playing basketball, he glided in comfort.

"Thanks. Those guys were rough. They were really shoving underneath."

"Yeah, but you were getting those rebounds. You were really hustling."

I felt like a nine-year-old who had just been told he had made the Hornets.

Robert came out of the shower, a cigarette somehow still dry and smoking between his lips. He was a rangy, balding man, a biology teacher, whose basketball talents were obscured by fat.

"Hey, who's coming to the bowling alley? I'll buy the first pitcher."

"About time you started showing some leadership, coach." John threw a wet sock at him.

"You guys don't need any coaching. Just greasing every once in a while."

"That mean you're springing for pizza, too?" someone shouted.

"Like hell." Robert looked at me. "What about you, Clary? You coming for a beer, or do you have to go home for a feeding or something?"

"I get a night off once in a while. Sure I'm coming."

The night air was still and freezing. The wet hair that stuck out from under my knit cap became encrusted with ice on the short walk between the gym and the car. We drove two miles down the highway and parked under a twenty-foot bowling pin, blinking red in the blackness. Tracking snow into the building, four of us settled into a booth near the jukebox.

"You played a good game," Robert said to me after we had ordered two pitchers of beer and some pretzels.

DADDY'S HOME

"Felt good. Thanks," I said.

"Basketball's a great game. Provides a good excuse to drink beer, and it keeps guys like Fast Eddie there from getting despondent. Right, Eddie?"

"The only time I get despondent is when I watch you play, coach. When are you going to lose some weight so you can get your butt up off the ground? That football player was leaping all over you tonight."

Robert waved away the insult. "Bulk," he said. "Modern game, you got to have it." He turned back to me. "So how do you like the life at home?"

"I'm enjoying it. I'm learning," I said.

"I had my kids for a while, when I was in graduate school. My wife was working evenings, so I'd have to feed them dinner, give them a bath, stuff like that. I liked it."

"You had two?"

"Yeah, twenty months apart. But they weren't all that much trouble."

"How long did you take care of them?"

"Oh, about nine months. I was finishing up my dissertation, and my wife was teaching elementary school."

"Then you switched back?"

He nodded. "She couldn't make any money, and she really missed the kids. She thought she might want to teach, too, but she was really into the kids."

Somehow, I was not finding this convincing. "She couldn't do both?"

"It didn't work out. But she's doing both now, now that we're divorced."

Robert screwed his face into an expression of resignation, and took a drink of his beer. "Anyway, I hear you're a writer. What are you working on?"

"Letters, mostly. I hope to do some free-lancing to maga-

A Man's Game

zines or newspapers, but I really haven't done much yet."

He looked surprised. "I thought you were staying home to write a novel or something."

"No. I'm really just staying home to take care of my daughter."

"Oh," said Robert.

He looked away. The conversation died. Eddie and Martin Widner began discussing country music. I pretended to listen, but I felt angry, alienated. Robert had said he understood, but he did not, any more than James Kirby or Roger did. Without committing themselves to a term as househusband, perhaps no man *could* understand that to take responsibility for the care of a child is to take *all* of it.

Pouring another glass of beer, I drifted into a Walter Mitty fantasy. I saw myself climbing up on the table and shouting for silence in a voice that immediately got it. "Kill that jukebox and listen up!" I imagined saying like John Wayne. "I'm a full-time father. Taking care of my baby daughter is what I do all day. It's my job. I am not a part-timer, a dilettante, a hen-pecked wimp, or a guilt-ridden husband giving his wife some relief from her natural duties so she can indulge a whim, or play career woman.

"Hell no! I accepted Annie as my job, to the exclusion of journalism, to the potential detriment of my career, at the expense of the money I could make. How's that for guts! I am serious about my work, just as serious as we are about playing basketball, or being college professors, or truck drivers or machinists. It's tough, dirty work, and anyone who doubts that hasn't tried it. All right now: any questions?"

There were no questions, just respectful silence. I resumed my seat and took another drink. There, I said smugly; that feels better.

"Hey, Clary! Snap to. A dollar fifty each."

DADDY'S HOME

"Oh, right," I said, blinking, reaching for my pocket.
"Come on," said Martin. "Let's go. Looks like you need some sleep."

My teammates and I never talked again about what I did all day. Where their occupations were acknowledged, mine was not. Where they could win recognition by making a comment in a faculty meeting, or by telling a story about their dealings with students, I could not.

I did not offer reports on Annie's progress in using a spoon to eat applesauce, or describe my exasperation over her spitting up strained peas on the beige curtain in the dining room. I did not tell them that sometimes what I remembered best about the entire day was the blissful moment of tranquillity I experienced when I lay down on the bed and knew that Annie was asleep, and would be for the next two hours. I did not presume. I did not dare. Maybe I should have.

When basketball season turned to spring, and we made the park a part of our routine, Annie and I took long walks. She would ride on my back, facing where we had been, babbling and exclaiming at people and dogs and cars and anything that caught her eye. On those walks we were advertisements for ourselves, inviting recognition. We were plain to see, declaring our partnership. I felt, as Roethke, "My secrets cry aloud./I have no need for tongue."

See us: I am a man, and she is a child. She is happy now, even angelic, but she can be a tyrant, imperious, demanding. She can wake up screaming in the night, or refuse to eat, or break lamps, or grow so cantankerous through a trip to the store that I whimper in frustration. She can be inscrutable, a maddening puzzle, and a wellspring of worry who breaks out into fits or rashes for no good reason. She can develop

A Man's Game

a cold out of sunshine and a warm breeze; her eye malfunctions, and I grow irritable when I think of it.

She can also cause me to blink back tears of love just by breathing deeply through an even sleep. For no apparent reason at all, I sometimes feel an outlandish sense of pride and love roll up from deep inside me, unbidden, like an accidental burp, and I step back from her in fear that I am about to suffocate the girl with attention.

The emotions Annie provoked frightened me at times. I had not known that I was capable of love that strong, or that paternal.

She grew, she learned, she prepared herself for walking. She was work. She required food, comfort, stimulation, and a lot of time. But by the end of ten months I knew that a man could handle the work of childcare. It was worthwhile, necessary work. Childcare was valuable labor, and it could be satisfying. It was labor that a man could perform and not feel it was trivial or demeaning or beneath his dignity. A baby could be man's work; a baby could be *that* important.

Chapter 12

The Blue-Mood Special

WHERE LILLIAN had business to attend to, I had chores. Where she had well-tailored suits and coordinated ensembles for office wear, I had T-shirts and blue jeans that were either clean or dirty. When she came home and told me that she would be going on a three-day staff retreat to a lodge noted for its gourmet food, I had a fit of envy.

"You'll be three days eating steak cordon bleu and asparagus vinaigrette, and I'll be here with Annie flipping SpaghettiOs at the dog," I loudly lamented.

"Well," said Lillian in an even voice that signaled her determination to avoid an argument, "do you want to go to Indiana?"

The Blue-Mood Special

"Indiana!" I said querulously. "I thought this exercise in indulgence was being held up north in some posh hunting lodge."

"It is. But two weeks before that I've been invited to Indiana to give a talk about the college career-development program. You could come along to that. Might be a nice change."

"And Annie?" I asked sarcastically. "What do we do with her?"

"Bring her."

"Some vacation," I carped. "It won't exactly be like leaving my troubles behind. Sort of a househusband's holiday, isn't it?"

"I know," said Lillian. "But the scenery will be different. You decide."

Accompanying Lillian to Indiana meant a five-hour car trip, and who knew what kind of inadequate overnight accommodations, while tending a rambunctious thirteen-month-old who had grown surprisingly strong-willed. With her full mobility and her burgeoning inquisitiveness and stubbornness, the decision to take Annie away from the familiar schedules and resources of home was not to be taken lightly. In fact, the more I thought about it, the more certain I was that a trip such as Lillian proposed was akin to agreeing to crew on a slow boat to disaster, a foolish blind mission to angst, frustration, and exasperation. Only a desperate man would accept it.

"Okay," I said. "But we've got to get a good meal out of this at least."

After more than a year as a househusband, almost anything that promised a break in the routine could entice me out of the house. Feeling numbed and becalmed by the confinement at home, I had begun to invest chores as ordinary as grocery shopping with an air of excitement. With

DADDY'S HOME

Annie riding shotgun in the shopping cart, we prowled the supermarket aisles like scouts on patrol, alert for movement under the exotic bunting over the foreign foods. We sensed the chill of danger in the freezer section. We rounded corners with quick stealth, tensed for action, ready to attack a mountainous display of canned goods. "Watch out for those green beans!" I whispered urgently to my partner.

Sometimes I deliberately underbought such staples as orange juice and cottage cheese, giving us an excuse to return to the store two days later. Steadily, the stuff of childcare and housework expanded to fill my days, if not my mind.

There were other telltale signs that I had begun to fray around the edges. Just days before Lillian's trip came up, standing over the washing machine sorting clothes, I realized I had begun talking to Annie's sleepers and lounge suits like they were family. "You guys sure got yourself messed up," I chided. "Well, I'm going to give you a good hot bath."

At lunchtime that Tuesday, I admitted to Lillian that my behavior had me worried. "You know that fuzzy pink sleeper with the rogue elephant on the front? Have you ever thought that it looks like a bowlegged homunculus, something like Jimmy Cagney in that dancing movie?"

"The *sleeper?*"

"Yeah, if you hold it up and move it a little."

"I hadn't thought about it," said Lillian, smiling, sure I was setting her up for a joke.

"You ought to take a look at it," I said.

"Are the sleepers talking?" Lillian wiggled her eyebrows like Groucho Marx, deciding it was best to play along.

"No," I said loudly, only partly in jest. "Even *they* won't recognize me."

Part of my frustration stemmed from my inability to complete a free-lance assignment. After selling the editors

The Blue-Mood Special

of the *Detroit News* on the timeliness of a look at the political militancy of conservative farmers in central Michigan, I couldn't seem to write the story. Using baby-sitters, I had managed to conduct interviews around the county and take dozens of photographs; but with my deadline approaching, I couldn't lay one word after another.

Although I seemed to have time (Annie's naps were now down to one—a minimum of two hours in midafternoon), I would find myself during that time sitting dazedly at the typewriter, typing nothing. I stared out the window, watching the sparrows, or catching a glimpse of Christine next door. The sight of Christine would set me to wondering about *her* ambitions, *her* mood, or what *she* was cooking for dinner. Sometimes I watched Nat, her son, with a towel safety-pinned around his neck, running pell-mell around the backyard yelling, "Sooo-per-man!" I marveled at his energy, and I tried to imagine Annie at that age. Would she play with the same exuberant explosion of energy? Would she run headlong and solitary, with such loud release? Would I be home then, monitoring her days? Would my days move more slowly as hers grew faster?

I became aware of cobwebs. When I couldn't concentrate on the paper before me, I looked up into the corners of the room and noticed wispy stalactites waving for attention. Standing on a chair to swipe them down with a handkerchief, I could then see that the ledges over the window frame and the door were covered with dust. Within minutes I would resolutely arm myself with a bucket of hot water and a spray bottle of ammonia and happily begin, cleaning not only over the door and the windows but the woodwork around them as well. It was good, satisfying work.

Sometimes, just emptying all the wastepaper baskets would do. I seized on any task that required a minimum of thought, and presented no chance of failure.

DADDY'S HOME

"There," I would say to myself, having bundled up the contents of all six wastepaper baskets into one plastic trash bag, "that's one job all finished."

Sometimes Annie was enough to keep me from writing, even when she was sleeping. I sat vacantly at the desk, the blank white page sticking up out of the typewriter with an insolent curl, taunting. When I could take no more, I would decide that I had better peek in on Annie, just to make sure. And, sure enough, she would be sleeping, just fine without me.

Of course, I couldn't write when Annie was awake, either. Two weeks after her first birthday she had blossomed into a toddler, tentative but full-fledged. With bipedal mobility, she changed both of our lives. Her world opened onto new vistas, and mine as a househusband just got smaller.

Annie's interest in exploration meant that I could no longer write when she was awake. She was not content to sit quietly looking through a picture book or playing with her blocks while I struggled to compose a memorable declarative sentence. She learned to climb. Her reach was elastic. She was insatiably curious. Leafing through catalogs of childcare products in the evening, I hoped to run across a moderately priced, expert-approved ball and chain.

In late September, when Annie careered through the house in a determined wobble and I was running out of patience, we packed for our overnight trip to Indiana.

The landscape in the upper Midwest comes under the influence of an alchemist in early fall and slowly turns to gold. We followed the interstate through fields of corn and yellowing soybeans, and then curled off onto two-lane highways that doubled as the main streets of small towns where the flag flew in front of stately white houses, holiday or not.

We stopped often. We stopped for gasoline, and at every other rest area, to trade off driving, and for drinks and

The Blue-Mood Special

snacks. When we unleashed Annie from the confines of the car seat, she toddled after birds and we chased after her, momentarily free from her demands for books and placation.

Along the way, I kept noticing other men in a variety of jobs that a year earlier I would have considered pedestrian beyond interest. Now, however, I was able to discern in these jobs the most striking attraction.

"You know," I said to Lillian after we had filled the tank, "working in a gas station along an interstate highway probably wouldn't be all that bad."

"Yeah," she said. "If you like minimum wages and lead fumes."

She kept her eyes on the road. Next to me in the back seat, Annie dozed upright.

"No, I'm serious. It wouldn't be that bad. Outside, meeting a lot of varied people, not real hard. Replace a fan belt, dump in some oil. Those guys get more than minimum wage. Hell, gas station owners are making a mint these days."

Lillian turned her head as if to make sure the voice she heard was coming from me. "You're not serious."

"I wouldn't mind being a farmer, either," I said as we sped by a red barn surrounded by an idle army of machinery. "There's a lot of satisfaction in working with the soil."

As I gazed dreamily out the window, following the path of a pickup truck that bounded down a lane across a distant pasture, Lillian decided to change the subject.

"I'm told this will be quite a comfortable apartment the college has for guests. And we can probably have a good meal, somewhere."

Around noon, the sun was obscured by a solid wall of thick gray clouds. Autumn masqueraded as winter, and the temperature began to drop in rapid clicks. By the time we found Woodside College, we all had our jackets on.

DADDY'S HOME

The campus held a hodgepodge collection of old red brick and sprawling three-story modern buildings that seemed to have been tossed down at random in too small a space. We could find no center to the campus, no way to begin to locate someone. Neither did there seem to be any place to park. When we finally did get in touch with Professor Vernon Meecham, Lillian's contact, I had begun to wish that Annie and I had stayed home, where we could content ourselves with a walk along the Pine River and a scheduled afternoon nap.

Lillian was to meet that afternoon with Meecham and several other faculty members to hear about Woodside's program in career education. Then, after an informal dinner in the cafeteria, to which Annie and I were invited, Lillian would speak to an evening faculty meeting on the subject of Bexley's project.

"You and the little girl might have a stroll around campus while all this business is going on," suggested Meecham, a stolid chain smoker who taught English.

Meecham gave us a key to the guests' quarters and a campus map. After twenty minutes of wrong turns, and another exasperating hunt for a parking place, we carried our suitcase, a jam-packed diaper bag, a sackful of toys, and Annie into a second-floor, two-bedroom apartment cluttered with worn Mediterranean-style furniture. A low-slung couch and three turquoise armchairs were all turned as if in homage to face a monstrous console television set wearing silver rabbit ears. On a coffee table were a glass vase crammed with plastic flowers and a year-old copy of *Aviation Week* addressed to a local doctor's office. In the adjoining kitchen I found four plastic plates, three coffee cups, a box of sugar, and several tea bags. A half-empty jar of mayonnaise had the refrigerator to itself.

The apartment had two bedrooms. The beds were firm,

The Blue-Mood Special

well blanketed, and long enough for someone five-foot-ten or under. That left me three inches too long. The small lamps on the dressers gave off a yellowish light; and against the gathering darkness visible through the blinds, the apartment seemed suffused with sadness. Dolefully, I considered the afternoon and evening ahead.

"No crib," I said to Lillian.

"I'll ask about one. But we'll probably just have to fashion a barrier out of something."

Annie had been known to bulldoze her way through makeshift barriers, but I refrained from complaining about that right away. More immediately, I wondered, how were we going to spend the afternoon leisurely strolling the campus when outside it was raining? Parting the blinds, I watched a cold drizzle drip from the leaves of the sycamore trees as Annie began to lick the dust off a plastic tulip.

After a quick lunch in the cafeteria, Lillian went to confer while Annie and I checked out the student union, the coffee shop, and the gymnasium, where, on a Thursday afternoon, not a ball was bouncing.

With Annie cranky and tired, we toddled to our apartment through the rain, and arrived wet. After getting us both dried off and changed, I was ready for a nap, but Annie was not.

"Time to sleep, kid," I told her. "Naptime, just like every afternoon."

"Naaaaawwh," she cried. "Booot, booot." She grabbed books out of the diaper bag, insisting I read her another story. One book led to another, and that led back to the plastic flowers again, and the knobs on the television, which she turned and twirled until even the interference lost its focus.

"Naptime," I told her again, while hauling her to the bedroom. I put her in the bed I had shoved into the corner, and quickly pushed the dresser up against the open side. She couldn't get over the top, but she could stand up in bed and holler.

At five o'clock, just thirty minutes after exhaustion had finally dragged Annie into sleep, Lillian came in and announced it was time for dinner.

"So soon?"

"Faculty meeting is at six-thirty."

Angry at being awakened, Annie was not fit company at the dinner table. The four faculty members who joined us in the cafeteria tried to ignore her continuous fussing, but I could not.

"She is not usually like this," I said to the bushy-haired man on my right as Annie poured her carton of milk on the floor.

"It's probably just the strange surroundings," he said, generously making light of the disturbance. "Lillian tells me you're a newspaper reporter."

"I was, yes."

"And you're staying home now, doing a little baby-sitting?"

"Well, you might say that," I said, wishing he hadn't. "I like to think of it as a little more than baby-sitting."

"Yes, I'm sure it is. I just meant, you're at home, giving your wife a chance to work. That's nice. She gives an impressive presentation."

"Yes, she's very good at what she does," I agreed. "Excuse me." I ducked under the table to mop up Annie's Jell-O with a napkin while imagining the same conversation about my performance on the job. Sitting upright again, I could feel the hot flush in my face. I felt ridiculous, even belligerent. Looking hard at my dinner companion, I decided to take it out on him. "Some of us are in the right business," I said.

The Blue-Mood Special

After dinner, I led Annie back to the apartment while Lillian went off to work. The rain had stopped, but a brisk wind had come up from the west, and knifed through my jacket with a chilling bite. Annie's nose was reddened, but as my spirits sank, she seemed to take heart. For the next two hours, she wanted to play, and I wanted to sulk.

At eight o'clock I gave Annie a bath and put her to bed behind a barricade of furniture. In defense against her cry, I turned up the sound of a mindless situation comedy and lay down on the floor and tried to make out the action from the ghostly shadows that danced behind the flickering cross-hatches flitting across the screen.

What *were* we doing here? What had made me think that this could be fun?

When Lillian came back at a quarter to ten, I had given up on the television, which had made me even more frustrated, and was lying on the floor staring at the crack that zigzagged down the middle of the ceiling. The sullen blackness of my mood must have been radiating through walls, for Lillian entered apologizing.

"Sorry. I didn't realize it would go so late. There were a lot of questions."

"It must have gone well, then," I said in a flat tone dredged in both my resentment of her good time and self-pity over my own plight.

"They were very interested," said Lillian. "But it was tiring. How did it go here?"

"Oh, it was eventful. Annie found some playing cards in a drawer, and ate a couple. Then she knocked over a lamp in the bedroom, denting the lampshade but somehow failing to break anything. We read books, played with the stacking toys, twisted the TV dials, and generally terrorized the place. She finally fell asleep about an hour ago."

"I'm sorry the weather isn't better. That could have made

all the difference." Lillian kicked off her shoes, sat down, and sighed. "Whew. I'm tired, too."

"I don't think the weather's the problem," I said, ignoring her complaint. "It's more than that. You have your work, and I have mine. My work doesn't have to be done in a strange apartment with no crib and none of the things we need."

I looked at Lillian accusingly. "You know what we forgot? Extra diaper pins."

"Did you lose one?"

"No, but I probably will," I said angrily. "Annie and I just should have stayed home. There is no reason for us to be here."

"We thought it would be a good break," Lillian said.

"But it's *not* a break," I responded loudly. I sat up to face Lillian. "All this does is remind me that you have business to conduct and I am just what that yo-yo at dinner said I was—a baby-sitter."

Lillian waited, avoiding my glare.

"No, *I* am the yo-yo," I continued. "You work the string, and I go up and down. Or to Indiana. Your schedule is our schedule. You *do* and we *wait.*"

Lillian kept silent.

"The idea that I am a writer as well as a househusband is a joke. You know that. I'm not getting any writing done, and taking on assignments just adds to the frustration. I just have to face the fact that I am not a writer now. Annie is a full-time job. And I am *just* a househusband; that's all there is to it."

Lillian stood up, removed her jacket, and hung it on the back of the chair. Waiting for her to speak, ready to pounce, I also stood up and began pacing. Lillian wandered into the kitchen and idly pulled open the refrigerator door.

"Mayonnaise," she said, as if to herself.

The Blue-Mood Special

"Yeah, mayonnaise," I said. "And do you know what that hundred and fifty I got for the last free-lance piece comes out to on an hourly basis? It's not minimum wage! And the aggravation! Who am I kidding? I have to learn to be content just doing a good job with Annie."

I was wound up now; my voice was rising, and I began to believe less and less of what I was saying. Stalking up and down the living room, gesturing grandly, I was an actor playing the role of a man whose patience had run out. I felt exasperated to the point of tears, and at that point I took the man's way out: I didn't cry, I got angry.

"I have been going around thinking I was Superdad or something. No. I'm just Adequate Dad. Full-time is full-time, right?

"Anyway, did you know what it would cost to duplicate the services of a homemaker like me on the open market?" I demanded. "Fourteen thousand dollars! I read it in *The New York Times*. So what the hell? That's what I'm worth; that's enough."

On a swing by the couch, I scooped up a fringed sateen throw pillow and absently began pounding it with my fist as I prowled. An invisible $14,000 was not enough; being a full-time househusband was apparently not enough; and the more I tried to convince myself that I should be content with only the rewards of childcare, the more ridiculous I sounded even to myself. But I was now committed to a self-serving tirade, an exorcism of malaise and frustration. I hoped that Lillian would interrupt me soon with an assurance that I was only normal.

At home I might have jogged around the block, or run to the tennis courts to smash tennis balls against the backboard. But in the cold confines of our guest apartment, I felt trapped. Pivoting after a length of the room, I whirled around and frisbeed the pillow back toward the couch, and watched it sail into the vase of plastic flowers on the coffee table. The vase skidded, then crashed to the hardwood floor, where the colors of the daisies and tulips looked obscenely bright against the white fragments of the vase.

"Damn!" I shouted. "Great! Let's trash this place, let's reduce it to rubbish! What is *happening* here?"

Retrieving the pillow from the tabletop, I slammed it into the corner of the couch, a can't-miss gorilla dunk.

"Who am I trying to kid? I knew what the job was before I took it on. I've read *The Feminine Mystique*. What did Betty Friedan call this? 'The problem that has no name,' right? So that's my problem. I don't know exactly what to name it either, but I am living proof that a man can have it, too."

I waited for Lillian to speak, to say anything. I was ready to attack whatever she said.

"Waxing kitchen floors is shitwork for women or men," I prodded. Was she going to get into this fray or not?

"Well," said Lillian, finally, slowly, the hint of a smile playing around her mouth, "maybe we should turn this househusbanding into a competition."

I glared at her. "What do you mean?"

"Men are taught to thrive on competition, to win for a sense of achievement," she said. "I'm that way, too. I have to have a goal. But at home with Annie, you never get any sense of how you're doing compared to others doing the same thing."

"There aren't any others!"

"Sure there are others. But we have to go national to find them."

"Oh, sure," I said, with as much dismissive sarcasm as I could muster. I sank down onto the couch, spent from my blustering tirade. "Like a bake-off, men's and women's divisions. Maybe a TV show. Three aproned men and, from behind the curtain, three squalling kids! Start the clock. How fast can these rugged homemakers change a diaper and get these irritable babies settled down?"

"Yeah," said Lillian, echoing the unctuous tone of excitement of a television quiz show host. "We'll call it 'Father Knows Best'!"

I began to laugh, even though I did not feel like laughing. Lillian sat down beside me and squeezed my arm. "You'd win," she said.

"Yeah, I probably would," I agreed, nodding my head rhythmically, smiling, realizing that I was not joking at all.

Although nothing about my role or my duties had been changed, I went to bed feeling more relaxed than I had in months. But I was not sure why. My outburst had apparently been cathartic, but I still did not understand what it was that had made me so depressed and angry in the first place.

I was, after all, a *volunteer* househusband. I was not caring for Annie because of anatomy, or tradition, or even necessity. When Friedan had written about the emptiness and frustration of women who felt trapped in unsatisfying, numbing lives as mothers and homemakers, she was talking about *lifers*. She was talking about women, most of whom had been conditioned since birth to sacrifice for their husbands and families.

Maybe that was the rub. I had not been conditioned for the life I led. My frustration was not rooted in gender, but in upbringing; my expectations were too high. Having tasted the piquancy of achievement and success in work outside the house, I could not be satisfied with the blandness of home. Many women, women like Lillian, also found themselves dissatisfied with the traditional female role. They, too, required jobs with more glamour, prestige, or status than housework. Many of those women, struggling to fashion a career in business while still managing to care for their

DADDY'S HOME

families, often were further burdened with unsympathetic husbands who never helped out with the children or the housework. There were, I knew very well, partners who never *understood*.

I, however, had in Lillian everything a beleaguered homemaker could ask for. She not only did a fair share of the housework, she assumed an equal responsibility for Annie. After work, and on weekends, Annie was as much Lillian's charge as she was mine. Lillian helped arrange for babysitters, did the laundry, took her turn cooking. She kept the Volkswagen in tune.

But even that didn't seem to be enough. Lillian's empathy with the hardships of my job, her willingness to help, did not earn her any inviolability from my outbreaks of self-pity, or any safeguard from my foul moods. She was an easy, convenient target. Resentful of her freedom to go to work, to escape the domestic malaise, often I would accuse her with sidelong looks and fits of sulkiness of not suffering her fair share. I was sure that many times she fled to the office in the afternoon wishing that, instead of spending the lunch hour with me, she had used the time to go to the library, or begin a fast. I could be very petulant. Sometimes, after a long day at the office, Lillian would return home to find me on strike.

"No dinner," I would tell her curtly when she walked in the door just after five o'clock. "I didn't get to the grocery store, and I forgot to get anything out of the freezer." I dared her to make something of it.

"Well, okay, do you want to go out somewhere?"

"There are always fish sticks," I taunted.

"Let's go out."

"What's the matter, don't you like my cooking?"

"Your cooking is wonderful. But I think we had fish sticks last night."

The Blue-Mood Special

"You don't *like* fish sticks."

"I *do* like fish sticks. But we have them a *lot.*"

We did. We had fish sticks and brown rice at least once a week, it seemed, and sometimes more often than that. The meal was my "Blue-Mood Special," a filler that required no effort and only a few minutes' forethought. On days when I felt particularly frustrated or sorry for myself, I used the meal as a weapon of assault. Sooner or later, I thought, those frozen bars of batter and mystery fish would provoke Lillian into battle. "FISH STICKS!" she would scream. "WHEN YOU HAVE ALL AFTERNOON TO SIT HERE AND THINK ABOUT DINNER, CAN'T YOU COME UP WITH SOMETHING BESIDES FISH STICKS!"

But she never did. She seemed to understand. She either ate fish sticks, and pretended she liked them, or insisted that we go out.

"These fish sticks aren't bad, are they?" I taunted. "I like a batter that's the same thickness but just a little tougher than the fish, don't you?"

"I'm so hungry, I could eat anything," said Lillian, deadpan.

"You're a saint, you know that?" I said.

"I am," Lillian said with a big grin. "By the way, what's the mercury content of these delectables?"

However frustrating and unsatisfying many of my days as a househusband were, I knew those days would end. After two years, Lillian would take over, and I could trade Annie's irregular summons for the predetermined ring of an alarm clock. I was not, like millions of women, settling into what I had been taught from childhood was a lifetime of adventure and fulfillment only to find it an incomprehensibly bitter disappointment. I was not a victim of the feminine mystique. So what was I bitching about?

I was not exactly sure of the source of the problem.

DADDY'S HOME

Although I had no reason to share a woman's sense of betrayal over the emptiness of the homemaker's dream, I felt it anyway. I wanted more. I did not want to give up staying home to care for Annie, but wanted *more* than that, too. As a journalist, I wanted time to write.

Driving back to Alma the next day, we began to work it out.

"The campus is full of potential baby-sitters," said Lillian. "We'll make a list of candidates, get each person's schedule, morning and afternoon. It seems quite reasonable to me that you should have specific times every day when we know you can write."

"But part of the problem is being at home," I said. "I sit there and think about the laundry, or the next meal, or picking up toys. Compared to the newsroom, you would think there would be fewer distractions at home, but it's worse."

"So we'll hunt for a place for you to work. Upstairs in the chapel, maybe, or a carrel in the library, or an unused office somewhere."

"It sounds wonderful," I said as we sped northward through Coldwater and Carson City. "Now if I can just avoid feeling guilty . . ."

In the rearview mirror I met Lillian's expression of wonder. Annie was on her back with her legs in the air. Lillian slid a fresh diaper underneath her bottom.

"You *are* joking, aren't you?"

"Yes. But I did take this on as a full-time job. I don't want to be copping out."

"Don't worry. There is no way you can cop out," Lillian assured me. "Annie is still your full-time responsibility. But I think we can make provisions for other needs, too."

"And it's not cheating?"

"Cheating on what? Your Superdad image? It's not a

154

The Blue-Mood Special

question of your competence or your commitment. You are not allowed to feel guilty. But you *are* allowed some time for other things besides childcare."

"Like time to write and adult companionship, right?"

"Right," said Lillian. "Like any housewife."

"Such understanding," I said, showing my renewed spirits in playfulness. "In appreciation, I'm going to fix you something special for dinner tonight. Fish sticks amandine."

"Please!" said Lillian, grimacing into the mirror like a person struck with a particularly horrible vision.

"Aha! You *don't* like fish sticks." I pounced with vengeful glee. "At last, an admission."

"No," she declared boldly. "I hate fish sticks. And I would like to call a six-month moratorium on eating them."

"Well," I said, "what an astounding turn of events. And what do you suggest I substitute for my Blue-Mood Special?"

"A trip to the Main Street Café," said Lillian. "It'll be healthier for everybody."

Chapter 13

Like Any Other Mother

WITHIN DAYS of our return from Indiana, I had found a vacant office on campus in which to work, and Lillian had helped me compile an impressive list of baby-sitters, complete with their class schedules, preferred working hours, and dormitory telephone extensions. With little effort, and no qualms, I was soon leaving the house at nine three mornings a week, just like a man with a regular job.

I finished the piece on farming for the *Detroit News* and took on another assignment to profile the University of Michigan's star quarterback. With my stalled avocation restarted, I felt like a serious free-lance journalist as well as a househusband. Writing regularly restored a part of me that

Like Any Other Mother

had been missing, a chunk of my identity, and the result was not only more pages of copy but a renewed enjoyment in my domestic chores.

As a bona fide part-time journalist, I spent less time nursing resentments over Annie's demands for my attention, and more time in awe over her gritty determination to mount an upright ascent of the stairs. We spent more time on the floor together, stacking blocks, looking at pictures, rolling tennis balls, talking seriously about the calls of animals. The house got cleaned more often, the laundry done more frequently. More imaginative menus were planned for a week ahead. We went entire months without once having fish sticks.

But I still did not have much of a social life. I was not exactly sure what kind of a social life my peers had, but I did occasionally see women and children come and go at Christine Butler's house next door. Were they having coffee? Wasn't that something housewives did? Were they in there gathered around some fresh-baked pastry exchanging hints on stain removal or effective discipline? Were they swapping recipes and tales, commiserating with one another, bucking each other up? Was there a cooperative association of homemakers that I had not heard about? I decided I had better find out.

"Do you ever get together for morning coffee, with the other mothers in the neighborhood, I mean?" I asked Christine.

"No, I never drink coffee," she replied.

"Well, I mean the coffee metaphorically," I said. "Don't you ever get together, just to talk things over?"

"Oh, like a therapy session," said Christine. "I talk on the phone quite a bit, and Barbara and I trade off watching the kids when we have to go to the dentist or do some special shopping. But just to socialize? No. Nobody has time."

"Ummm," I said, mulling that over, thinking: *I* have

DADDY'S HOME

time. Why is that? What should I be doing that I'm not?

"Why?" she asked. "Do you want to get together for coffee some morning?" She smiled, making a joke of it.

"Not coffee," I said. "Not if you don't like coffee. Maybe a beer."

"Oh, sure!" said Christine, as if surprised by the suggestion. "Wouldn't Dick love that."

"We won't invite him," I said conspiratorially.

"Oh, sure!" said Christine again, louder this time, frightened by the thought of it. "Sure."

My chance to mingle with others in jobs like mine came one Saturday when Lillian ran into Lamaze classmate Sherrie Cooper at the bank. Sherrie mentioned a weekly play group that she and several other mothers had begun.

"It gives the kids time to play with others their own age, and the mothers have coffee," Sherrie said. "I know you work, but if you'd like Annie to come, I could pick her up."

"It sounds great," Lillian said. "I'll ask Mike."

The chance for Annie to meet other toddlers, and play in a group, was immediately attractive. Although we tried to get her together with other small children as often as possible, at fourteen months she was a clinging vine, and I was her trellis. She needed all the socializing she could get.

I did not consider joining the mothers for coffee until Sherrie telephoned to confirm Annie's participation. I had answered the phone, but although she knew full well that I stayed home with Annie, Sherrie asked to speak to Lillian.

"What did she say?" I asked, smarting slightly at what I felt was Sherrie's discourtesy.

"She offered again to pick up Annie. But I said you could take her over."

"Why? Do you think I should stay?"

Like Any Other Mother

"Do you want to?"

"I don't know," I said, trying to sort out my ambivalence. "Did she say anything about my staying?"

"She said, 'Mike could stay if he wants to, but he probably wouldn't find the conversation very interesting.'"

That struck me as a reasonable assumption. I needed the time to write, anyway. The conversation probably would be boring. The play group was for the children, not for the parents. I didn't think I did want to go.

Or did I?

"You could just take Annie over there, to Carol's house, and see what happens," Lillian suggested in a way that indicated she thought I should. "If it's interesting, stay."

Sure, I thought. I could go with the option of staying. And who knows? It could be interesting, or even fun. Perhaps I could learn something. Perhaps I could make some friends.

On Thursday morning I dressed Annie in a turtleneck sweater, overalls, and tennis shoes, and we drove to Carol's house on Lawton Avenue. The sun fought valiantly to push through menacing banks of high, dark-gray November clouds, succeeding in klieg-light flashes.

Walking up to the front door, holding Annie by the hand and carrying a diaper bag over my shoulder, I had still not decided whether I wanted to stay or not. I was curious about what the morning would be like, for both the children and the adults, but at the same time I hated to pass up the chance for two or three hours alone at the typewriter.

Carol, whom I had met only once before, answered the bell with a friendly smile, opening the storm door just wide enough to stick her head out into the chilly morning air.

"Hi," she said.

DADDY'S HOME

"Good morning."

She reached down and took Annie's free hand. "Hi, Annie," she said warmly. "You want to come in?"

As Annie haltingly stepped over the threshold, Carol looked up at me and extended her right hand, palm upward. I looked at her dumbly, thinking she wanted to shake hands.

"Extra diapers?" she asked.

"Oh, yes," I said hurriedly, swinging the bag off my shoulder and handing it to her.

"She'll get along fine," Carol said confidently. "Why don't you come back about eleven-thirty?"

The door closed and I found myself slowing walking back to the car before I fully realized what had happened. Not only had I not been invited in for coffee, I had not been invited in to say hello. Telling myself that I didn't want to come in anyway did not seem to mitigate the hurt.

From home I called Lillian at work.

"Did you tell Sherrie that I didn't want to stay for coffee?"

"No. What happened?"

"Well, I was a leper at the gate. I wasn't even invited to decline."

"If you want to stay, maybe you have to be more assertive," said Lillian.

When I returned at 11:30, Carol reported that Annie had gotten along fine, just as predicted. "She fit in beautifully," Carol told me. "Can she come again next week?"

"Yes. That would be great."

"At Betty Simmons's house."

"Fine. And I think I'll be finished with the little project I'm working on, so I'll be able to stay, too."

"Oh," said Carol, her oval face opening in surprise. "Good."

Like Any Other Mother

Between that Thursday and the next, the pique that I felt at being summarily turned away from Carol's door like a bill collector with bad breath had been overwhelmed by my desire to get inside the play group. Just like a man, I rose to the challenge. Cracking the inner sanctum of the play group had become a contest, a goal; within, perhaps, lay the secrets of motherhood, knowledge of mythic proportion, never revealed to a man. Somewhere in that kaffeeklatsch was to be found the wisdom of the race, the answers to questions I had not even thought to ask yet. I *must* get inside.

Never mind that all I had was a case of loneliness, that all I wanted was a little communion with others in my line of work. Never mind that, as a full-time keeper of a child and a home, I thought I *deserved* to be admitted. Never mind that I honestly expected no such magical or mystical revelations. The game was on.

Just as Lillian fought tokenism to gain a place in a man's world—she was one of only two woman administrators—I would have to struggle to integrate the female world of home and children. Our only difference was gender. All else being equal, was that too much to overcome? Did they doubt my commitment to homemaking? Did they question my sincerity or competence? Didn't they think I was as interested in my child as they were in theirs?

I *would* have coffee and cookies with the mothers. And I would make the cookies.

On Betty Simmons's front porch that next Thursday at nine, I delicately wielded a shoe box full of double peanut chunkies like an aromatic passport, and made my intentions unmistakably clear.

DADDY'S HOME

"I thought we could all have a cookie with our coffee this morning," I said to Betty, the willowy, soft-faced wife of a doctor. Betty backed into the house as I steered Annie over the threshold and wedged in behind her like a brush salesman. "Peanut butter," I smiled.

Betty took the cookies while I unwrapped Annie and ushered her into the dining room. Three small children were rummaging through a toy box, while two others pushed wheeled animals around the table. Annie sprang away from me and hauled herself aboard a rocking horse.

I joined Sherrie and Carol and two other young women in the living room while Betty went to pour me a cup of coffee. Sherrie made the introductions.

"Mike is Lillian Buchanan's husband, and Annie over there is their little girl. This is Jane and Cassie, and you know Carol."

"Hi," I said, sitting down on the raised red brick hearth.

Jane turned to Carol and picked up the thread of a conversation that the introductions had severed.

"Well, anyway, we had a lot of trouble over that tire because Jed was sure that it was defective—tread separation or something—and the manager claimed it was glass. Finally, Jed just exploded. I guess he got red in the face and was shaking with anger. He said he would ask Ron Allen over at the Ford dealer to stop dealing there, and, oh, he was upset. But we finally got forty percent credit on a replacement."

"That's the third horror story I've heard about them," said Carol, shaking her head in disgust. "You have got to get tough with them."

"Jed did," Jane averred. "I'm just glad I didn't have to deal with it."

"No, I don't like those confrontations either," said Cassie. "But I'll stick up for my rights."

Like Any Other Mother

"Oh, you've got to, you've got to," added Jane. "Nobody else will look out for you."

I had been following the conversation, gaining some first impressions, settling into the ambience of the gathering without being struck by anything in particular to contribute on the subject of tires or how to deal with merchants. I disliked those confrontations, too, but agreed with Jane that you had to stand firm. Suddenly, aware of a lull in the conversation, I got the discomforting impression that it was now time for me to make my first kaffeeklatsch remark. The subject of tires seemed spent.

Slowly swiveling my head around to take in all of the living room, my gaze lingered on a dangling chandelier, and I said to no one in particular, "This is a nice house."

My observation commanded a stunning silence. In the next room, even the children seemed to grow quiet.

"Yes, very comfortable," Cassie finally said.

For what seemed like minutes, I continued to scan the room, searching for inspiration. No one spoke until Betty came in with a cup of coffee and a platter.

"Mike made these," she said, setting a mound of multi-shaped lumps on the coffee table.

"Oh, wonderful," said Jane, picking a cookie off the plate. "You bake, too, eh?"

"Well, I try a few simple things," I said. "But I don't think I have any special talents."

"I understand you stay home with Annie," said Cassie. "How is that working out?"

"Pretty well," I said sincerely. "I'm enjoying it."

"And your wife's at the college, right?" asked Carol. *There*, I thought, now I have been defined as they were—through my spouse's occupation.

"Yes, she's associate director of the career-development program and a counselor."

DADDY'S HOME

"Yes, I think I've heard of her," said Cassie. "Carol, you know Dr. Howard's wife, Jenny? She mentioned she'd heard Lillian speak."

"Oh, yes," said Carol, the light of recognition in her eyes. "How's Jenny doing? She was having a hard time with her pregnancy, wasn't she?"

Over the subsequent two hours we talked about hand-me-down clothes, the necessity of heating an infant's food to suit adult taste, the looming winter, styles of strollers, how to find a good pediatrician, the grand opening of a discount store, the average waiting time for the public library's copies of best sellers, and the monolithic football season and its effect on the family.

At the mention of football, the group turned to me, almost as if signaled by a tone audible only to the ears of women.

"Yes, football," I said, thinking of the story I was working on, and deciding not to mention it. "It really is popular, isn't it? Lillian likes football."

The five women looked at me without expression. I sat forlorn, like a spy who had slipped up.

"I think football is stupid," said Jane, and the conversation drifted onward.

I heard enough about each woman's husband to know what they all did for a living, and form an impression about their general disposition. I learned that Carol's husband, William, was allergic to a particular brand of detergent; and that Cassie's husband, Pete, allowed no one—not even his wife—into his woodworking shop in the basement.

With only occasional fits of jealousy over toys, or outbursts signaling wet pants or more mysterious discomforts, the children played together like a team of tender champions. Betty put on a Sousa record and we all marched around a cardboard box in the living room. I helped Annie

Like Any Other Mother

and a new friend named Nicholas with a puzzle, and Carol took some photographs of all six children crammed inside a wooden rocking toy shaped like a boat.

I had three cups of coffee, two cookies, and well before 11:30 I began to wish I had spent the morning at home writing.

Driving home, I realized that I felt much the same way that I had felt driving home the week before: rejected. I had been admitted to the house, but, once inside, I was still an X among O's. My presence had served to drive the women closer together, to impel them to take stock of their similarities. The exchange about football had hammered home my difference, turning me from just another concerned parent into a stereotype, a token of all men. I was *with* the group, but I was not *in* the group. I had not integrated the club after all.

As I unbuckled Annie from her car seat, Christine pulled in next door with a load of groceries. Nat and Douglas bailed out of her car, whooping.

"How are you doing?" she called.

"Fine. We've been over playing with some other little ones this morning."

"Sounds like fun. You, too?"

"Of course," I said emphatically. "I joined the other mothers for coffee."

"Aha," said Christine as we walked toward each other. "Passing on your secrets, huh?"

"I don't have any secrets. Anyway," I added, feeling no hesitation to confide a little in my neighbor, "they didn't ask me for any. I don't think they figured I had much homemaker's wisdom to pass on."

"They don't know you like I do. They don't know you're serious."

I laughed. "Yeah, well, I would think that would be obvious. Annie's almost fifteen months old, and I have taken to measuring the days in terms of naptime and loads of laundry."

"That sounds like what Dick would call empirical evidence," Christine chuckled. "Did you tell that to the mothers?"

"No."

"They probably wouldn't have believed it anyway. You just don't look right. I think it's the beard."

Back home, over lunch of chicken noodle soup and crackers, I continued my lament. Lillian seemed sympathetic, but was unsure of my specific complaint.

It was not clear to me, either. "I just thought that a kaffeeklatsch would be more interesting. I thought there would be some serious discussion about being a mother, or a housespouse. I know that men don't talk about personal matters, but I thought women did. I don't know, maybe I expected an encounter session."

"Did you bring anything up? Anything personal?"

"I mentioned Annie's eye." We both looked at Annie, who was finger-painting on the tray of her high chair with a mixture of applesauce and cottage cheese. Under her eyes were puffy, dark half-moons that made her look like an insomniac. "I said the condition worried me. That was sort of a confession, don't you think? But there was no real response. Most of the time I felt like I was inhibiting the conversation, and at other times I felt like the invisible man."

Lillian spread cream cheese on a cracker for Annie, and then looked at me thoughtfully.

"I think the women may have seen you as the oppressor. They are together for mutual support as women. The children are theirs. They gave birth to them, and they are in charge of them, and they know them. They *have* to be there.

"But you? They don't know what you're doing. You may

Like Any Other Mother

be slumming, or writing a novel for all they know. They don't know your credentials. They can't really believe you're as sincerely committed to being a father as they are to being mothers. *They don't know that you have anything to say about childcare.*"

"Well, why wouldn't they know that?" I grumbled. "I'm doing the same things they are doing."

"Ah! Except for one thing. You're a man. You know what it's like?" Lillian's eyes brightened. "It's like the routine when we go to the auto-parts store and the mechanic insists on directing his questions to you, even when it's clear that I give the answers."

Oh, *that* routine!

I hated working on cars. I did not fully understand how they worked; and when they stopped working, I immediately suspected either sabotage or bad karma. Along with my mechanical ignorance, I had virtually no mechanical aptitude. I relied on Lillian to keep me on the road.

Lillian loved working on cars. She understood the internal-combustion engine, and appreciated it. She kept our Volkswagen in tune, changed the points, plugs, condenser, and oil, adjusted the valves and the brakes, and, with help, had even pulled the engine and replaced the clutch. Although I tried to duck her orgies of car maintenance, occasionally I had to serve as tool caddy or brute strength.

Often in the midst of repairs we had to make a trip to the auto-parts store. When Lillian went alone to these strongholds of masculine expertise, approaching the counter in overalls and wearing grease like a second skin, she usually got friendly, courteous service, the right part, and all the earnest advice she could carry. The man behind the counter was bemused by the idea of a woman fixing her car. Lillian was no threat to him as the possessor of knowledge, and he handed down tips gladly.

DADDY'S HOME

I was greeted differently. As a man, I was presumed to have some expertise in auto repair. I might also be presumed to be a serious challenge to the clerk's authority.

When Lillian and I went into the store together, confusion often ensued.

"We need a solenoid for a 'sixty-five VW," Lillian told the man.

"Is it a 'sixty-five six or twelve volt?" the man asked me.

"Six, but I think the solenoid's the same," Lillian replied.

The man looked at me skeptically and threw open a huge book on the counter.

"You need a new pinion gear?" He glanced up at me fleetingly.

"I don't know," I said, turning to Lillian.

"No," she answered, "but we did bend the retainer and ring clip pulling off the starter, so give us one each of those, please."

With that the man looked up, first at me, and then at Lillian. "What about a pivot pin?" he asked, looking straight at her, acknowledging the real competition.

"Got one," said Lillian, smiling politely.

The man behind the counter finished writing up the order, and then turned to fetch the parts, unsure if I was truly an automotive dunce, or if Lillian was really as mechanically savvy as she seemed.

I understood his bewilderment. We were like a comedy team, playing for laughs the reversal of sex roles. He was uncertain how to take us. What was certain was that gender no longer told him quite everything about his customers.

I never returned to the play group. Even though I received several compliments on my double peanut chunkies, and even though I was confident that with persistence I

Like Any Other Mother

could overcome the awkwardness of that first visit, I did not want to go again. Once home, I realized that the two and a half hours at Betty's house did not constitute one of the rewards of childcaring, but served instead as one of the consolations. The group brought together mothers with similar concerns and interests, perhaps, but the convention would not provide me with any insights into being a parent that I could not gain alone at the typewriter. The mothers were company—and I wanted company—but those women were not like me. Amid their talk of husbands' jobs and supermarket specials and cute antics of lovable children, I would find neither the companionship I craved nor the path to enlightenment. I was not sure what, besides company, I was looking for, but I knew that cake and conversation with the mothers was not the way to find it.

When Sherrie called the following week, I again answered the phone, and she again asked to speak to Lillian. "We're going to meet at my house this week," she said. "Does Mike want to come with Annie?"

"I think he'd like to bring Annie, but I don't think he'll stay himself," Lillian said.

"Oh, fine. It's probably boring for him."

"No, it's just that he has some writing to finish, I think," said Lillian.

"I understand," Sherrie insisted. "Our little group gets hectic sometimes. Not really a man's type of party."

Chapter 14

The Sneakers' Lament

WAITING FOR WINTER in Michigan is a cat-and-mouse game. By the middle of Annie's second November, we had grown edgy. For weeks the cold had toyed with us, hugging the distance, threatening from the wings. Afraid to pass up a single day of grace, Roger and I continued to play tennis under the pale sun. We wiped sweat from our brows and looked over our shoulders. We were ready to quit, to change seasons, but the sky remained clear.

When winter finally did steamroll over the stubborn Indian summer, it came in with startling fury. We woke up to a gray tuck-and-roll sky and a sharp wind that rattled the windows. Late in the morning I dug my goosedown jacket

The Sneakers' Lament

out of a box, put Annie in a quilted red snowsuit handed down by a cousin, and we walked over to the tennis courts to wonder at the transformation.

The high branches of the white pines danced wildly; the wind whipped around the corner of the football stadium, noisily piling leaves up against the green fence. The wooden benches where the day before Roger and I had sat to catch our breath had been overturned like insects, legs in the air. Fine points of snow briefly swirled about us, stinging our faces. Annie's eyes watered. As we ran along the baseline, chasing an empty tennis-ball can being rolled by the wind, two college custodians pulled up in a truck and began to take down the nets.

In the afternoon I put my tennis racket in the closet and found the Pistol Pete Maravich autographed basketball in the basement, nested in a stack of snow tires. I dribbled through the kitchen and sat on the floor to roll the ball to Annie. "That's it! Basketball!" I cheered when she thumped it with her open palm.

On that first hard day of winter, Lillian came home from the office thinking about basketball, too. A women's intramural league was being formed. "Exercise! Fun! Excitement! Thrills!" she beamed, taking a bounce pass in the dining room. "I haven't played basketball for years, but I remember it as something like controlled frenzy."

"Frenzy?"

"Well, a game that gets you so involved that there is no time to think about planning the parent-involvement conference or wonder why the computer program didn't run."

Lillian had the right perspective on athletics: They promote exercise and teamwork. She never thought about winning. Nevertheless, competitive basketball was a tough game to sell to professors and secretaries several years away from their limited experience with sports. Many had no experience with sports at all. But eventually, Lillian collected a roster of ten women who promised to show up at the gym once a week for an evening of fitness and fellowship.

Lillian also sold college president Swanton L. Williams the idea of donating $50 for team shirts in exchange for the honor of having the team carry his name. In a postpractice meeting in the bowling alley lounge, the team was christened "Swanny's Sneakers." A few weeks into the season, when the Sneakers' prospects had become painfully clear, rumor had it that Williams was willing to pony up another $50 if the team were renamed, and his sponsorship never again mentioned.

The Sneakers' problem, simply, was that most of Lillian's teammates had never played organized basketball before; and those who had played did not play very well, at least not in comparison to their undergraduate opponents. Some of the difference between the Sneakers and their competition could be explained by age or height or energy, but the telling contrast was experience. The Sneakers did not have much. Furthermore, Lillian and those teammates who had played basketball before had been told that playing hard was unladylike, and were therefore taught to play by "women's rules," a set of Victorian strictures apparently designed to save women from unfeminine exertion. Under those rules, half the team was prohibited from shooting the ball or leaving their half of the court.

The players on the other teams carried no such handicap. They knew how to play. They had been taught to play basketball like men and boys are taught. They played aggressively, with quickness and confidence. The students handled the ball with sure hands, drove hard for the basket, shot with practiced touch. The Sneakers may have been the best-dressed team in the league, uniformly outfitted in blue numbered jerseys, but they were also the humblest. The scores

The Sneakers' Lament

of the first few games were stark testimony to the character the Sneakers were developing: They lost the first three games fifty-four to two, twenty-eight to four, and thirty-six to nothing.

Annie and I went to the first few games. She was not at all interested in watching basketball, but the foldout stands beckoned as Mount Everest had to Mallory: They were there. I tried to keep one eye on her and one eye on the game, but I soon gave up. The basketball game was not something I was able to enjoy, anyway.

In those first three games, the students took the ball away from the Sneakers almost at will. Some of Lillian's teammates, when stripped of the ball, would look to the referee, throw their hands in the air, and, in perfect frustration, plead for redress. "It just doesn't seem fair!" they would cry, stopping to bemoan their haplessness while the other team stormed back down court for another easy lay-up.

It *didn't* seem fair. After struggling so hard to dribble the ball from one end of the court to the other without once bouncing it out of bounds off a foot or a knee, it did seem an injustice not to be able to get close enough to heave the ball toward the hoop. But it happened time and again.

Even after vowing to keep my mouth shut, I would find it opening in exasperation. "Run, Carolyn! You have to get between her and the basket! No, not *that* basket!"

Finally, I gave up watching the Sneakers play basketball. The games left me more than frustrated; they left me angry. I identified with the team, and was humiliated by the weekly drubbings. Half the Sneakers didn't seem to understand the rules; or, if they did, they became too rattled during the action to obey them. They dribbled with both hands at the same time; they walked with the ball; they repeatedly tried to pass through defenders. The team's best player, Jenny

Howard, whose husband was our family doctor, was in her last trimester of pregnancy through most of the season, and yet she still ran faster and played harder than almost anyone else on our side.

Jim Howard sometimes acted as the Sneakers' coach. Normally imperturbable, even Jim became agitated with the Sneakers' inability to move the ball past half-court. "Pass!" he shouted, leaping to his feet. "When you can't dribble anymore, pass!"

"Jim, I bet you don't get this excited for a coronary arrest," I told him in the midst of one game.

"I know what to *do* for coronary arrest," he said.

Lillian, too, became frustrated by the ineptness of some of her teammates, especially the hapless, dotty refusal of some of the women to play aggressively. But she maintained the perspective she had come in with, a perspective that saved her from quitting in disgust. She was able to remember that the team had been organized for the sake of camaraderie and exercise—and against that measure, the Sneakers were a success.

In the stands, however, although I had the time and the distance for the historical perspective and, like Lillian, knew it was only a game, I got angry anyway. I couldn't help myself. With not even a generation between Lillian's team and the students who ran them dizzy, they were worlds apart on the basketball court.

After one midseason game, with Lillian and her teammates at the bowling alley for a postgame beer, and Annie in bed exhausted, I brooded in the study. After skipping through the newspaper, becoming even angrier, I began a letter to disperse my frustration.

> Having just returned from the bullring, where Lillian's basketball team was once again gored, this time twenty-six to six, I didn't

The Sneakers' Lament

need to read a column by William F. Buckley, Jr., to put me in an anarchist frame of mind, but I read one anyway. And although it was predictably aggravating, it does serve to buttress my case for girls who sweat. Buckley says, "Really, the feminists have gone too far," because they want to be drafted along with men. He says allowing women to fight wars would destroy their natural "charm." He then quotes Dr. Sam Johnson to make his case that charm is an ennobling gift bestowed on women by men. Women "are less vicious than we," said Johnson, "not from choice, but because we restrict them. . . ."

Surely it seems like folly to struggle for the right to fight a war. But after ninety minutes of Sneaker basketball, I am for doing away with charming for women, certainly by the time that Annie grows up. Charming is frustrating. While Lil's teammates were striving to forget themselves and play ball, on the other side of the gym two women students tossing a baseball back and forth made a revealing tableau. These two knew what they were doing. They fired the ball at each other with smooth, sure ease and nonchalance. They played ball like—well, like boys. And watching them, so graceful, made me happy. There, I thought, were two young women who at least in one part of their lives were not going to be denied because of some man's notion that women should be kept charming.

I hope Annie is not so charming that she cannot play ball. I hope she doesn't have to go to war either. I have visions of her being able to read and write, and run and sweat, and even be considered attractive in the eyes of her peers. But, boy, I hope she can hit the jump shot from the top of the key, too, right over Bill Buckley's outstretched hand.

One night in January, weeks after I had given up Sneaker basketball for the sake of my blood pressure, Lillian and Susan Vander walked in the front door with their tennis shoes under their arms and what I thought was a surprisingly smug expression on their faces. They looked almost as if they had won a basketball game.

"Guess what!" beamed Lillian. "We won!"

"You didn't," I said.

"We did," affirmed Susan. "We clobbered them."

" 'Clobbered'? The Sneakers clobbered somebody? Somehow I can't picture the Sneakers committing an act like that."

"Maybe 'clobbered' is too strong," allowed Lillian. "But we won decisively, how about that? Sixteen to twelve."

"Wonderful," I said tentatively, still tending to treat this news with a full measure of journalistic skepticism. "How did it happen?"

"We got a new player," Lillian confessed as she and Susan plopped down on the couch. "René Price, the new women's physical education teacher. She scored twelve points."

"And Lillian got two and Jenny got two," added Susan.

"So she knows how to play, huh?"

"Yep," said Lillian proudly. "She brought the ball down the floor, we passed it around, and then she either took the shot or put in a rebound. It was wonderful."

"We are getting better," said Susan. "You ought to come back and see us."

"Maybe I will. But do you think I should bring Annie? I don't want her overexposed to too much of a bad example. She's at an impressionable age."

"Very funny," said Susan with a smirk. "By the end of the season, we'll be good."

The Sneakers never got to be good, but they did get better. Annie and I returned to the games, and, as she wandered in the corner of my eye, I watched the action on the floor and monitored my anger. Sometimes I sat and talked to Jim, who had given the coaching job over to the team's new star, René Price. Jim and I talked about basketball, of course; and Ohio, where he, too, had grown up; and, eventually, Annie's eye.

The Sneakers' Lament

"What's MacGregor say about that?" he asked me, looking at the swelling under her right eye.

"He thinks it'll have to be operated on," I said.

"How old is she now? Fifteen months? Probably better do it. One-eyed basketball players have a hard time making a major college team or the NBA."

That was a man's joke: Annie as a potential candidate for the National Basketball Association, as if we could determine her value or her future by measuring her athletic prowess. I not only understood the joke, I had told it many times myself. But suddenly the joke rang hollow. We were no longer talking about women as professional basketball players, or sexism, or even paternal expectations. We were talking about Annie's health, and an anxious fear rose from my stomach. Had I made a mistake? Had my concern for her eye infection been too casual? Had Jim misled me with his calm assurance that the condition was not uncommon and would clear in time?

"You think we ought to go ahead with it then?" I asked Jim, looking hard into his eyes.

"It's a very simple procedure," he said.

I turned back to the game, but I could no longer concentrate on the play. It was time to face up to a truth as cold as the winter wind that quickened our steps between the gym and home: Annie would have to have surgery.

Chapter 15

Fear and Surgery

I HAD first taken Annie to see the ophthalmologist when she was nine months old, and the doctor had left me cold. Malcolm MacGregor was an angular, austere man who spoke with measured precision. Like Jim, who had recommended him, MacGregor struck me as unflappable. He projected a clam professional competence. But in the few words he spoke, I never sensed the empathy that made Jim so easy to talk to. He never showed me that he had a sense of humor, and that bothered me.

MacGregor examined Annie while making a soft clicking noise designed to distract her. He seemed distant, impersonal, uncommunicative. After a cursory look at her eye with

Fear and Surgery

a light, he told me flatly during that first visit that the tear duct would have to be "surgically probed." I didn't want to hear that.

"Can't we continue with the drops, and massage? The left eye eventually opened."

"You can," he said impassively, dourly, as if he were used to tolerating fools.

"What's the danger of it not opening?"

"Infection. Could lose the eye."

"What! Really?"

He looked at me sternly and tilted his head in the slightest of nods. "Not going to happen right away, but it could."

"Is there any point in waiting any longer to see if it will open?"

"You can try another three months if you want."

I wanted. The idea of submitting Annie to surgery and an anesthetic made me shudder. Surgery was traumatic. Anesthetics were drugs that could burn out brain cells. Accidents could happen.

We kept after the eye, but it would not clear. Many mornings, Annie still woke up half-blind. Futilely, we squeezed in drops, and massaged with our little fingers. The three months of home therapy stretched into six.

"I remember my aunt Nell saying that one of her kids had the same problem," Lillian said. "But it never got to the point of an operation."

"I know. Even Spock says it's fairly common, not serious."

I called Jim Howard. "What do you think?" I asked him again.

"I would respect MacGregor's opinion. He's a good doctor."

"He has always seemed like such a cold fish to me," I said.

"He runs marathons," said Jim. "He's not the backslapping type, but I've never heard his judgment questioned. I'll be there for the operation if you want me to."

We returned to MacGregor's office for what was called the "pre-op examination." Annie would undergo outpatient surgery the next morning at the same hospital in which she was born. As I held her on my lap, MacGregor leaned in behind a thin ray from a pencil flashlight, scrutinizing her eye. Annie toyed with a ring of keys he had handed her, oblivious to the lurking danger, or my mounting concern.

"Should be a simple probe," he said, as casually as he retrieved the keys when Annie threw them down. "You should have her at the hospital by six-thirty."

"Now remind me again of what's going to happen," I said. "I just want to be clear. . . ."

"I will insert a tiny wire probe into the corner of her eye, break the membrane in the tear duct, and that will be about it. Flush it a little. Ten-minute operation."

"And she will be unconscious?"

"Oh, yes. She can't be moving around."

"And the anesthetic?"

"Ketamine, probably."

Probably? That sounded so offhand. Didn't he know *exactly* what anesthetic, and *exactly* what its effects would be?

"Ketamine," I repeated. "Is that a standard . . ."

"Yes, a very common anesthetic. She will recover completely from it in hours."

We stood up, and, with Annie in my arms, we walked out of the examining room toward the receptionist's desk. MacGregor was making quiet clicking noises and winking at Annie.

"How common is this operation?" I said, still groping for a more basic appreciation of our situation.

"It's not something that most children have, but I have

Fear and Surgery

done it many times. It's a fairly simple procedure. Rose will give you some forms to read and sign. We'll see you tomorrow."

The doctor winked once more at Annie, and then disappeared into the examining room with his next patient, an elderly man with thick bifocals. I could see MacGregor steer him into the chair before the door closed.

Rose handed me a pen and a form: "Consent to Operation, Anesthesia and Other Procedure." Six paragraphs of legalese that said, in effect, that I recognized the dangers inherent in the surgical procedure to which I had agreed, and that accidents could happen. I set Annie down, and she scooted back into the waiting room and pulled the blocks out from under an end table. I stood staring at the paper, pen poised. MacGregor had been so casual, so blasé about the operation, but this waiver of liability sounded so stark, so threatening, so coldly malevolent.

One phrase bothered me: " . . . and I completely understand the ordinary risk involved and the possibility that complications may arise." I didn't feel that I did *completely* understand. I read the phrase out loud, inviting Rose to comment. She did not look up from a ledger on her desk.

"I think I'd just like to check this with the doctor," I said to Rose.

"You'll have to wait till he comes out," she said, flashing me a perfunctory smile.

I waited. I knew I would have to sign the form, but I still felt I was missing some key to understanding what it meant. How *much* risk? *What* complications? Spock, in *Baby and Child Care*, alluded to surgery, but he made it sound no more dangerous than a haircut. "If by a year it is still bothersome," he said of the obstruction, "an eye doctor may clear the duct with a simple procedure." Why did the language in the form make the operation seem so much more serious than that?

When he emerged from the examining room, MacGregor seemed surprised to see me still there.

"Excuse me, doctor, but I just wanted to clarify this one paragraph. I don't think I do completely understand the risk and the possible complications."

"Well, this form is necessary for all surgeries, large or small. The eye probe is, as I've told you, a simple procedure. But any time there is anesthetic involved, there is some risk."

"Some risk?" I repeated.

"Some, yes." His quiet voice had acquired a bite. "But I have never had an adverse reaction to ketamine. Is that what is troubling you?"

"I just want to fully understand. I know you have done this operation dozens of times—"

"And never had any complications," he added quickly.

"—and never had any complications. But you have never performed this operation on *my* daughter. I am just concerned, that's all."

"I understand that," he said, adding emphasis to his patience. "What is it you want to hear?"

"How dangerous is it?"

"The worst that can happen?"

"Yes."

"It is possible that she could go to sleep and never wake up."

Knowing what was coming did not lessen the shock. MacGregor smoothed his lank brown hair and waited. From the corner of my eye, I saw Rose look up, holding on to an inhalation of cigarette smoke. A wave of queasiness broke in my stomach.

Was *that* what I'd wanted to hear—that Annie could be

Fear and Surgery

injected with an anesthetic and then die? I stared at MacGregor. "Anything else?" he seemed to be asking. "Are you satisfied?"

"Okay," I said. "Thank you."

Shaken, I bent to the form and signed my name. MacGregor turned away as a cloud of acrid smoke drifted down over my head. I felt nauseated.

Picking Annie up from the waiting room, I hurried outside and sucked in large drafts of fresh air. How absurd, I thought, that I had just thanked a man for telling me that my daughter could die the next day on an operating table. And I had just signed a paper saying I understood that! But wasn't that what I had asked for? I had prodded MacGregor until he admitted it! Annie could go to sleep and never wake up. Or she could lapse into a vegetative coma, and live forever on spoonfuls of Pablum.

I drove home in a daze, horror movies going around like thirty-second loops in my mind. Aunt Nell's kid avoided this operation. I had never even heard of this problem a few months ago. Spock says that in most cases these tear ducts open even if nothing is done. Why did this have to happen to us?

Pulling into the driveway, I shook my head to untrack the bad dream. Annie tugged at my hair as I unbuckled her from the car seat. At the window, Katydog barked an excited hello, her front paws bouncing on the sill. Now I knew; I had chased the ghost of possibility into the darkest corner. Annie might not wake up. Knowing that should make me grateful, even relieved. Now I could not be surprised. Now I would not be a parent who had never asked.

In the afternoon I talked out my fears in a letter to my parents:

DADDY'S HOME

I've had two operations, right? Tonsils out when I was eight, and then a hernia operation when I was about eleven, if I remember. Actually, I don't remember much. I don't remember my fear, or your anxiety, or, I imagine, the studied friendliness of the doctors and nurses. I remember only the rewards for enduring, the prize I would get on the other side. For the tonsils I got ice cream, all I could eat. For the hernia I got a baseball glove and the assurance that I would be able to play again almost immediately. Those things I concentrated on so hard that all else is blurred.

If I carry any psychic scars today, any festering sense that you abandoned me or caused me unnecessary pain, I am unaware of them. And now that I am about to give up Annie to surgery, my experience should be some comfort to me. It may be *some* comfort, but it's not enough. She is too young to understand what is going to happen, and she is too young to dwell on any reward I could offer. And what could she want? More mashed banana and jelly sandwiches? More sleep? More time in the bathtub? No.

After Annie's operation, I have decided to reward myself. I shall gorge myself on chocolate mocha ice cream and buy a new baseball glove. I am feeling better already.

That evening I went to the college library and looked up ketamine in the *Physician's Desk Reference*. I thought the more I knew, the less I would worry. But after reading through the description of the drug and its effects, I worried that I knew too much.

"The stuff sounds just like LSD," I reported to Lillian. I read to her from my notes. " 'The psychological manifestations vary in severity between pleasant dreamlike states, vivid imagery, hallucination and emergence delirium. In some cases these states have been accompanied by confusion, excitement, and irrational behavior which a few patients recall as an unpleasant experience.' "

"Annie is too young to make all those connections," said Lillian. "I think you have to have a head full of imagination to bad-trip, don't you?"

Fear and Surgery

"It does say the reactions are slightest in the very young and very old," I admitted. "But I wouldn't want to take it."

"You don't like to take aspirin either. If you have to be sedated tomorrow, I'll make sure you get something you're used to—peanut butter, maybe."

"Perhaps I'll just overdose on reality," I said, "and pass out from apprehension."

With a diaper bag full of toys and books, and our hearts full of misgiving, we arrived at the hospital before dawn. I felt like a Judas, delivering my child into the cold hands of medical science. "This will hurt me more than it will hurt you," I repeated over and over, like a mantra. I wanted to smile over the irony of making a Hail Mary out of such a ridiculous platitude, one I had heard often as a child myself. But I just didn't feel up to smiling.

Even at six in the morning, the emergency-room entrance was pungent with disinfectant and nervousness. In my arms, Annie was placid, unconcerned. "Trust me," I wanted to say. "Trust your daddy. It won't hurt. Afterward we'll have ice cream. I'll buy you a baseball mitt. It'll be okay."

We were assigned to a room in the children's ward to wait for MacGregor and the anesthesiologist. In the bed by the door, a chipper young girl in a white hospital gown was sitting up coloring.

"My name's Jocelyn," she said brightly. "What's her name?"

"Annie."

"She going to be in this room?"

"For a little while," I said.

"How old is she?" asked Jocelyn.

"Almost fifteen months."

Annie poked around the room, opening drawers, then fishing scraps of construction paper from the wastepaper basket by Jocelyn's bed.

"She can have that," said Jocelyn. "Is she going to have an operation, or what?"

"Yes, on her eye," said Lillian.

"They'll probably come and get her at seven-thirty. That's what time they always come."

Jocelyn's precociousness unsettled me. She spoke with the bored certainty of a longtime Death Row inmate. I looked at my watch and wished for the day to be over.

Lillian put Annie in a hospital gown and began reading books to her.

I asked Jocelyn what grade she was in.

"I should be in fifth, but I think I'm going to miss this year. I have a friend here, down the hall. Her name is Missy. She had open-heart surgery."

"Really?" I said, shuddering slightly at the thought of such a big operation on a child so small.

"Yeah, and another friend, Beth, she has cancer. Hopkins disease, or something like that."

"Ooooh," I said sadly, and sat down to wait.

MacGregor never did show up. But precisely at 7:30 a stout man dressed in a gauzy space suit, wearing a cap and face mask, appeared and asked for Annie Buchanan-Clary. Could I have denied she was there?

Bravely, I turned her in. Lillian handed her over. The anesthesiologist said, "Dr. MacGregor will see you in the waiting room right afterward."

He boosted Annie to his shoulder and walked out of the room, singing in her ear, "Good morning, good morning." Lillian and I stepped into the hallway and watched forlornly as our daughter's enlarging blue eyes disappeared through a swinging double door.

Fear and Surgery

"It's a simple procedure," I said. "He's done it dozens of times."

"She'll be fine," said Lillian.

"He's never seen a bad reaction to ketamine."

"She is not as worried as we are," said Lillian.

"You know," I said, turning to Lillian, "I felt this same helplessness the last time I was in the hospital, when she was born."

We had a cup of coffee in the cafeteria before going to the waiting room to put in our time. At that hour, no one else was there. From her bag, Lillian pulled out a book on "the conflict theory of decision making." I riffled through stacks of creased magazines. A drawing in a June 1978 *Time* caught my eye. Two grotesque parents, flanking a worried Dagwood dog, were shrieking their concern for a bawling toddler who had climbed a ladder to the top of a plateau. The plateau was the top of a block representing eighteen months of age. The illustration accompanied an article on a book called *Oneness and Separateness,* in which a psychologist described a child's "second birth" as an individual apart from his or her mother. To effect this psychological birth, the author, Louise Kaplan, suggested children, especially girls, at an age between ten and fifteen months, be discouraged from clinging to their mothers.

Maybe the operation would benefit more than Annie's right eye. I liked the idea of a developmental bonus.

"Have a look at this," I said, passing the magazine to Lillian. "Annie's not only getting her eye fixed but being born again."

"You mean she's going to have a religious experience?"

"No, I mean this psychologist says she has to make the break from us to become independent. She'll probably be a lot less demanding when we see her again."

Lillian scanned the article. "Well, the operation may be

a part of the separation process, but I don't think Annie will remember it at all. *We'll* have the scars."

"I hope," I said. "But I'll take any silver lining I can get. I just don't want this operation to be the sort of betrayal that causes her to run away from home at thirteen."

Lillian read on, and then looked up at me with an abrupt "Ha!"

"Did you see this line: 'The father's role in a toddler's life is important but subsidiary'? See, that probably skews the whole theory in our case. The assumption is that the family is the normal one—father working, mother at home with the baby."

"So what does that mean in our case?"

"Who knows? It probably just means that Annie will become herself."

Once Annie was out of sight and the operation was under way, I stopped fretting and began believing she would return to us with the same number of working brain cells she'd had when she left. I had tended her eye, collected information, quizzed the doctor, and then, when there was nothing more I could do, I had let her go. We had decided not to ask Jim to be there. We trusted MacGregor.

A few minutes after eight, I looked up and saw in an instant that our faith had not been misplaced. MacGregor, striding across the waiting room in his green surgical gown and cap, showed the most expressive look I had ever seen him wear. He was actually smiling.

"She's fine," he said. "She's in the recovery room now. You can meet her back in Pediatrics about noon. She is conscious, but groggy. She needs to be kept quiet."

"So everything went all right?"

"Fine." MacGregor took a small pad of paper and a pen from a pocket under his gown, and drew what looked like a thin worm, and then beside it an eyeball. "This tear duct

Fear and Surgery

here was blocked by a membrane. I slipped a probe up there, punctured the membrane, and opened the duct. The block was just where I thought."

"And that should do it?"

"It is possible that it could become impacted again, and we'd have to reopen it. But chances are slim."

Now we were able to eat breakfast. In the cafeteria I felt playful. "You know what I should ask MacGregor? 'Doctor, will she be able to play basketball after the operation?' And he says, 'Sure, of course she can play basketball.' And then I say, 'That's funny, she couldn't play before.' "

Lillian winced. "And MacGregor will say, 'Henny Youngman, nineteen forty-seven.' "

At noon, Annie was carried back to the room. She looked dazed. "She looks like she got hit in the head with a board," said Jocelyn. But she knew us; she seemed to be whole.

Two hours later, after we had read *A Walk in the Zoo* and she had clucked and growled in all the right places, MacGregor examined her and said we could leave.

"Bye, Jocelyn," said Lillian. "I hope you get to go home soon."

"Yeah, probably not. But there is going to be a movie tonight. Cartoons."

"Great," I said. "Have fun."

At home, Annie began slowly, but within an hour was tormenting Katydog, scaling the door and the window ledge to watch the boys next door throwing walnuts at their wagon, clamoring for more books to be read aloud. She showed no signs of trauma.

Lillian went to her office, and I stood over the stove, stirring a chocolate pudding mix, waiting for molten bubbles. Internal bleeding, heart surgery, cancer; that wrongs so monstrous could afflict children seemed unfair.

Annie pulled the pots and pans out of a kitchen cupboard,

the only one without a safety catch on the door, the one meant for her. I left the wooden spoon in the pudding, violating the package directions to stir constantly, and bent down to hug her.

"How are you, little bean?" I looked in her eyes; they seemed clear, a vivid blue-gray. She pulled a roasting pan onto the floor, and climbed into it.

"Putt," she said. "Putt."

"That's right, pot. Those are pots. Isn't it good to be back home in our own kitchen!"

Chapter 16

The Classroom Carnival

ONCE EACH SEMESTER the three of us became an exhibit, trotted out for display before twenty-five college juniors in Sociology 312, Marriage and the Family. The professor, Margaret Holder, was a trim, dark-haired woman of fifty-five who had been teaching for three decades. She was an earnest, conscientious teacher who did not tire of her subject, in part because she was adept at spotting in the college community's shifting tides any irregular waves. Margaret saw in us more than just friendship; she saw lecture material.

"You," she told us gleefully, "are the best live example of

the nontraditional family I have ever had. You people are not even in the textbooks yet."

Although Lillian enjoyed the classes, and had no reservations about candidly discussing with strangers the assumptions and particulars of our lives, she viewed our visits to Margaret's class chiefly as favors for a friend. Lillian was a credentialed professional, with a position, plenty of work, and the respect of her colleagues. She did not need any more attention or recognition. She did not need confirmation as part of a family of some unique sociological significance. But I did.

To me, the invitation to offer up our lives as a classroom show-and-tell was an irresistible bit of carnival. Our day at school was part evangelism and part freak show, but all academically legitimate. Lillian was not an ordinary working mother, nor a career woman who had simply farmed out her child. And I was not an ordinary man stuck at home with a baby while unemployed. We represented something more, a family of revolutionaries. And now, after months in the nursery, I, a volunteer househusband, endlessly rocking, ever serious, was available to talk. At last, I thought to myself immodestly, on one afternoon each semester, we reaped the serious recognition that was our due.

We made our debut in the classroom when Annie was not yet three months old. I pulled a sweater over my T-shirt, dressed Annie in a carefully chosen aquamarine lounge suit, wrapped her in a knit blanket, and carried her across the street through a spitting rain. Lillian came down from her office on the floor above the classroom and met us in the hall.

As the students filed in, Margaret directed us to right-handed desks pushed up against the green chalkboard. Annie, her rash in timely remission, lolled in a plastic carrying seat on the table between us.

The Classroom Carnival

I was a little nervous. Unused to being on such formal display, and unsure what kinds of questions or reactions we would provoke from a roomful of upper-middle-class twenty-year-olds, my voice quavered when I first spoke. But as in our baby shower, the air of awkwardness made the audience eager to laugh at the most weak-kneed joke. When Annie abruptly emitted a loud squeal, I turned to the class and deadpanned: "That's the sort of behavior that keeps us from getting invited out much." The laughter steadied me.

Bexley College students typically come from comfortable Republican homes in the suburbs of Detroit, and they reflect the conservative beliefs of their parents. They are high achievers. The curriculum they follow is solidly liberal arts, but most students are prudent enough to know that for every class they take in romantic poetry or sculpture, they need to take some accounting and business management, too. After graduation they did not join the Peace Corps or hit the road; they bargained with Dow Chemical Company for a salary and a future, or went straight to dental school. I did not expect to be hooted from the room when we revealed the heretical details of our lives, but I was prepared for skepticism and surprise.

The first class, like the shower, began stiffly. The students peered at us from a distance. They seemed wary of getting involved. Margaret had to ask most of the questions. The few students who did want to know specifics of our arrangement asked how we settled on Annie's name, or which one of us balanced the checkbook.

The highlight of that inaugural appearance was a noisy, eye-popping performance by Annie, in which for fifteen minutes she held the students spellbound as she filled her pants. Accompanying herself with a virtuoso improvisation of grunts and squeaks, she strained in rigid concentration, the color rising in her face, her fists and her gaze clenched in exertion. At first only a couple of the young women seated near the front of the room seemed aware of the drama unfolding before them, but as Annie's solo grew louder, the entire class became caught up in the action. Titters of embarrassment gave way to awed appreciation for the elemental struggle taking place; and when Annie at last relaxed in satisfaction, a ripple of applause ran around the room.

Had there not been a half-hour of class time left, I would have waited to change her. But Margaret made a joke of it, and Lillian protested that dressed as she was—in a light tan jacket and skirt—she could not possibly get involved. The class seemed to come alive at the prospect of seeing me engaged in a task so fundamental to my role. With the students huddled around us at the table, I felt like a biology professor working over a frog. As I mopped up and rediapered her, Annie was radiant from the attention.

None of our later appearances included such a practical demonstration of a man's ability to master a basic requirement of childcare. But the discussions did get livelier.

Usually Margaret began the class by introducing us, first by name and occupation, and then as grist for the sociological mill.

"Many of you know Dr. Buchanan from counseling and career development. And you may have seen her husband, Mike Clary, and their daughter, Annie, on campus.

"You'll remember that on Monday we were talking about the family—the basic, conjugal, nuclear family, the primary social unit—and some of the ways it is evolving to reflect changes in values and shifts in culture.

"What is the *function* of the family? To provide emotional security, to provide the foundation for the individuals to play out their cultural roles in the larger society, to facilitate the raising of children, and to transmit the culture to those children, right?

The Classroom Carnival

"But when the institution of marriage, and the family, comes under attack by forces from industrialization to feminism, then the family must respond with change. In this family," said Margaret, indicating us with a wave of her hand, "the father is not economically dominant, and the mother is not dependent. The division of labor into male and female tasks, once so clearly defined in our culture, has been blurred. Dr. Buchanan has the *instrumental* role usually played by the man, and Mike has the *expressive* role usually played by the woman.

"You might wonder, what are the possible effects of this switch on Annie's psychosexual development? Is this an *egalitarian* marriage or simply a *matriarchal* marriage? What *cultural* values will this family pass on?"

The first time I heard Margaret's introduction, I was stunned. Was she talking about us? I could not have answered any of those questions. Hearing a roomful of students asked to ponder Annie's psychosexual development made my head spin. Was that sociological double-talk, or something we should have figured out long ago?

Fortunately, the students did not seem to want the answers to those questions. They were more interested in who did the cooking, and what would happen if Annie Buchanan-Clary married a man who also had a hyphenated name, and *they* had a child. "Would their baby have *four* last names?" wondered one bemused student.

"I guess that will be for Annie and her husband to work out," I said. "I hadn't really thought about it."

"Do you think you should have?" the student asked, to the accompaniment of laughter.

Lillian and I joined the laughter, and that served as our response.

Despite Margaret's introductory prodding, the students were always more concerned with the practical problems our

DADDY'S HOME

arrangement posed than they were with theoretical threats to Annie's future development or our feathery assault on the fortress of convention. The students, thinking ahead to their own jobs and marriages and families, wanted to know how we as a family *worked*.

The novelty of a baby in the classroom was in itself enough to hold many of the students in thrall. I imagined that for a young woman fascinated with the sight of an infant contentedly toying with a ring of keys, it was almost impossible to think of that child as a potential victim of personality disorder.

Only once, on our last of four appearances, did I carry Annie out of the classroom feeling anything but exhilaration over the chance to talk about ourselves to students who were generally interested in and approving of how we lived our lives in the red brick house across the street from campus. Only once did I feel challenged by a person in the classroom who seemed to believe that what we were doing was wrong.

Annie, at eighteen months, had been running around behind Lillian and me, scrawling in chalk on the bottom edge of the board while we fielded questions about our household chores.

"We don't have a budget as such," said Lillian. "Our money all goes into one account, and we pay the bills, and we either save what is left over or we spend it on a movie and a baby-sitter. We are not very organized that way."

"What about housework?" someone else asked. "Who does what?"

"Again, that seems to have fallen into place without much organization," Lillian continued. "Mike does the dishes, because he says he doesn't mind doing them, and I do most of the laundry."

"She does all the laundry that she wants to come out the same color that it went in," I said.

The Classroom Carnival

From the back of the room came a man's voice. That in itself was unusual. More than ninety percent of the students in Marriage and the Family were women, and the male minority was habitually silent.

"As a man," he said, eyeing me with a tough sideways look, as if following something out the window at the same time he talked to me, "how do you think you're benefiting the cause of women's liberation by doing work that everyone agrees is less important than what you might be doing?"

I reached for a clarification. "You mean, do I think what I'm doing benefits women's liberation—"

Margaret interrupted. "Bob, I think you're asking Mike about the equity theory, right? If housework or childcare is valued less than journalism, in Mike's case, won't he be considered less successful than a housewife who becomes a journalist, for example? Is that right?"

Bob nodded, his eyes locked impassively on mine.

"I am not familiar with the equity theory," I said hesitantly. I was certain that an accusation had been made, but I was still struggling to pin it down. "But I am not staying home as a blow for liberation, although it may work out that way. In our particular case, it was just the most appropriate way our family could be set up. But I am aware that I get a lot more attention for doing the tasks that women normally do, just because I am a man. And that helps."

"He can get the attention, but not the credit," Lillian interjected.

"That's not what I mean," said Bob. "I mean, don't you ever feel unmasculine?"

"No," I said immediately, smiling. When my answer hung in the silence, I felt compelled to say more. "No, I don't," I added.

What else could I say in a few minutes before twenty-five strangers who may have been looking at me like a sideshow geek? Did Bob and his classmates really want to hear about my childhood, my parents, my notions of self-confidence, my views on work and morality, my weltanschauung? Could I extemporaneously describe, without sounding silly or saccharine, my magical partnership with Lillian? Without seeming self-righteous or supercilious, could I hope to explain to the class why I did not share their undergraduate dreams of status and money and career success?

No. I just said no. Take my word for it: I do not feel unmasculine caring for Annie. Perhaps if I had thought myself a failure at being a househusband, *then* I might have been plunged into an identity crisis. But with this child as my witness, I think I am doing well as a full-time father. Her robust, lively good health attests to my success. I decided long ago that being a househusband was work worthy of me. I don't feel unmanly. I feel like Ferdinand Magellan; I have learned to sail right through the fog of accusatory questions like that.

"Maybe I could explain a little more by adding this," I finally went on. "Having been home with Annie for a year and a half, I know a little about what millions of women have known very well for centuries: that childcare and housework do not always add up to a complete, nourishing career. But at the same time, there are satisfactions in this work, and I have learned how to savor them for all they're worth. If nothing else, I have learned how to wring every ounce of stillness from an afternoon nap. I have learned to talk "kids" in the check-out line at the supermarket. And I've seen this kid here do things that I still don't understand.

"But as long as men are denied the chance to be househusbands—because it's considered unmasculine—they are being discriminated against as surely as are women refused entry to the top levels of business. When Annie is

The Classroom Carnival

an adult, I hope it will be possible for her and men her age to choose any work, inside or outside the house. And I hope there won't be any stigma attached to either."

"And if she chooses to be 'just a housewife'?" asked Margaret coyly.

"We'll disown her," I growled.

The bell rang as if on cue. The students funneled through the door, many of them stopping to have a word with Annie on the way out, or to touch her head or hand. Margaret thanked us for coming.

"I always enjoy being a part of the family of the future," I said. "At home it's sometimes hard to remember that we are an evolutionary advance."

"Well, you know," said Margaret, turning serious, "most of these students don't believe you really are a valid model. Although only seven percent of all families now fit the image of the traditional American household—working husband, full-time housewife, children at home—most high-school and college students don't approve of a wife working to support a nonworking husband."

"Sometimes I don't approve of it either," I said. "I'd like to go back to work—I'd do anything—but Lillian won't let me."

"That's not true, Margaret," protested Lillian. "I permitted him to come here today, and I *know* there is housecleaning to be done. But we have a liberated marriage."

"Or you could think of it this way," suggested Margaret. "You may have the only kind of marital arrangement that allows Mike to have an important role." She grinned wryly at me. "If Lillian has the job, and as a woman she has the children, too, what is there for you to do?"

"Just the dishes, I suppose," I said.

"Exactly," said Margaret. "So isn't it lucky that Lillian has given you some real responsibility?"

DADDY'S HOME

"Yeah," said Lillian, echoing Margaret's ironic tone. "Aren't you lucky?"

"I sure am," I agreed, bending over to catch Annie as she made a pass by us in the hall. "Now if you'll excuse me, I'm going to take my child and go home to work. I wouldn't want to lose this job."

Chapter 17

The She-Bear in Me

EACH MORNING I fished from the lawn a reminder of where I was, and what I was missing. Our newspaper came by truck from Detroit, but it could have come from any large American city. The *Free Press* was chock-full of crime and politics, international headlines, celebrities and comics. In a small town like ours, abuzz for months over a street-widening that meant relocating the Tastee Freeze, a big-city daily was like the spoor of some formidable beast that kept just out of sight. Skipping through the news while drinking the first of two cups of strong coffee was enough to turn up my small-town tranquility into a steady drone of anxiety over the future.

DADDY'S HOME

Some days going through the newspaper made me want to go back to the newsroom and wrestle with a reality of more cosmic significance. A compelling feature story could make me feel like a bench warmer itching for action. On other days I would come up out of the "A" section for air, see Annie playing with her Cheerios, and feel grateful for the distance between my circumscribed world at home and the strangeness beyond. I was torn by a familiar ambivalence.

The daily newspaper did not cause me to grow dissatisfied with my lot at home, or make me appreciate my time with Annie less, but it did remind me of a former, disparate life. Lillian and I had casually agreed that I would stay home to care for Annie for the first two years while she worked, and then we would switch roles. The evaluation study that Lillian was doing as part of her job was nearly completed, and although she had been offered an extension of her contract at Bexley, she was ready to move. The newspaper reminded me that it was time I began looking for work as a reporter.

"What do you want for Mother's Day this year?" Roger asked me one day in early May. We were sitting on the front step watching Annie drop stones into a bucket of water.

"Oh, just candy, flowers, and a job," I said.

"A job! For two years you've been telling me you *had* a job. I was just starting to believe it, and now you're telling me you don't have a job?"

"I mean a *new* job. One that produces a paycheck."

"You're going to leave? When?"

"June, maybe."

Roger picked up a stone that had rolled up against his shoe and handed it to Annie. We both stared at the sidewalk, our forearms on our knees.

"Who am I going to beat at tennis?" he asked.

"I don't know. I don't know if there is anyone else in town you can beat."

The She-Bear in Me

Annie swirled her arms in the water, giggling as the spray hit her face. A cool spring breeze stirred her fine blond hair. I would not let her play in the water too long, I thought, lest she catch a cold.

"I thought you had this childcare business down, and were enjoying yourself?" Roger looked at me. I sensed in his tone of voice a note of disappointment, as if I had betrayed him.

"I do enjoy it. But I don't want to make a career of it. I don't want to stay out of newspapering too long."

"You know, you've been home with Annie so long now, it doesn't seem strange anymore. Susan and I were talking about when we might have a kid, and I realized I was thinking about staying home, too. It surprised me!"

"Really?" I thought he was joking. But he wasn't. "Great. That's great. You'd do well. You'd like it."

"What would I like?"

"Staying home with a baby."

"But what particular parts would I like?"

"Oh," I said, looking up at Annie, whose shirtfront was now a deep wet red, "times like this, watching the kid play. Just feeling very close."

"What else?" he said, challenging me to come up with more.

"Ah—well—I like giving Annie a bath, watching her play in the water; reading books, making animal noises. I like to tickle her. Giving her hugs is wonderful."

Roger looked at me questioningly, still dissatisfied.

"I don't know," I said. "It's just hard to describe."

"Apparently," he said.

When Roger left to return to his office, I felt like I had let him down. Not only were we planning to move away, leaving him without a tennis partner and a potential role model, but I had not been very eloquent in describing the joys of childcare. They were hard to pin down. In the study I had a file folder full of newspaper and magazine articles in which mothers offered paeans to homemaking and childcare. Most of them, I thought, came off as defensive and flat.

In one article, a report from a New York conference on housework sponsored by the *Ladies' Home Journal,* a Brooklyn mother of seven was quoted as having "insisted" that she loved being a housewife because "no other job would give me these rewards. There is no pay, no medals, even, that could bring me this feeling."

Unfortunately, the article did not go on to spell out just what feeling the mother from Brooklyn had in mind. At the time I read it, soon after Annie was born, I thought the feeling she referred to was probably fatigue. Later, I was sure it was frustration she meant.

Another mother, this one living in South Nyack, New York, with her five children, defended homemaking as creative, fulfilling, ennobling work. She wrote that she did not find her duties any more boring than, she imagined, brain surgeons found theirs. She added that she had clout as a housewife because "(forgive me, Gloria Steinem); I sleep with the boss."

And just days before my exchange with Roger, I had clipped a Mother's Day tribute from the *Christian Science Monitor* in which a northern California housewife recounted a horrifying afternoon filled with inconsolable children, broken-down appliances, and loneliness and then added, apologetically: "Sure there are frustrating moments. But it is worth it to be home for the good ones." But she did not go on to list the good ones.

There *were* good moments. Those I had served up to Roger were good moments—quick, diaphanous flashes beamed straight to my heart. But they were ineffable; they

The She-Bear in Me

didn't translate well. Clearly, the women from Brooklyn, South Nyack, and northern California had not passed along any sense of what they experienced. They had been too defensive. Childcare and housework often *were* boring. Some days I would have been cheered immeasurably by a medal. The work was frequently frustrating. Admitting that all was not bliss did not constitute heresy in my house.

On the sidewalk, a rivulet made its way across the grain of the concrete and turned sharply right into a crack. An ant climbed up into the sunlight, escaping the flood. Maybe, I thought, I should have told Roger about the afternoon several months earlier when Annie and I met the woman in the black cloth coat in Jim Howard's waiting room.

Annie had been on my lap, chewing on the strap of the diaper bag. She was seven months old and due for her third inoculation against diphtheria, polio, and tetanus. I disliked these visits in which I had to hug her to my chest and distract her while a nurse snuck up behind and jabbed a needle in her thigh. Her reaction always came on a three-second delay, as if she could not believe that I had permitted someone to cause her the pain she felt. "Whhhhhy?" she demanded angrily through her tears.

Like any parent, I delivered her into the coolly efficient hands of the nurse because I loved her, because I did not want her to catch a disease. And like any parent, I was grieved to do it. I sat with my arms around her, wistful, aware of a faint aroma of shampoo in her hair, when the woman in the long black coat came in and sat down opposite us. She was carrying a thin young boy who was wearing high brown shoes. She put the child on the floor at her feet and pulled off his jacket.

Jim's waiting room was long and narrow, the size of a trailer. Everyone sat close together. When the woman looked up, I nodded to her in silent greeting. She had a

DADDY'S HOME

worn, lined face. I judged her to be about fifty, a country woman.

"What is he, about fourteen months?" I asked. The child had crawled underneath the seat to collect several plastic blocks.

"No." she said. "Almost two. He's small. My grandson."

"Oh," I said, thinking that the child's size or health was not an inviting topic to pursue. "He's a good-looking boy."

The woman looked down at her grandson, as if to confirm my judgment, and then softly said, "Yes."

Annie continued to gnaw on the cloth strap while watching the boy intently. "She's seven months," I said.

"Seven months," the woman repeated. In her dark eyes flickered a faraway look, as if the words had prompted a deep reverie. After a brief moment, she returned her attention to me. "When he was seven months, I thought he was going to die."

The stark, expressionless look on her face confused me. "Really?" I asked, concerned.

"When he was that age, he was half her size. Puny child, nothing to him. He was born premature, then got an intestinal-tract infection. Couldn't eat. In an incubator for two months, and no bigger than a blind pup."

She lowered her eyes to the boy, who was painstakingly lining up the blocks on the linoleum floor.

"When my daughter brought him home, he weighed less than seven pounds. I didn't think he'd make it. I never counted on him. I'll tell you the truth: I lost one of my own many years ago, and I was afraid to get too attached to this one. I thought it might be easier. . . ." She paused, remembering.

"But the child had courage, God love him. He's going to make it. And now . . ." She looked up to me again, her eyes brimming with tears. "And now I'd kill for him."

The She-Bear in Me

I thought the woman was going to cry, but she blinked and looked down to the floor. Then I blinked. A tightness rose in my throat. I pulled Annie closer to my chest, and tilted my head until her hair tickled my nose.

Kill for him? What a strange, startling expression, I thought. I could not imagine saying that myself as a way of indicating my love for Annie. But yet, I knew exactly what she meant. I, too, felt that she-bear protectiveness, an all-encompassing concern for the welfare of my child that never abated.

The woman across from me in the waiting room was a mother and grandmother, and I was a father. Neither of us had given birth to the child we cared for, yet we shared a love for our children that was usually described as maternal. It was a love that transcended gender and biology. The act of caring, of assuming the responsibility for our children, linked us in a mutual understanding. Nothing was more important than the child we cared for; and in providing that care, we had constructed a love of awesome power. Yet her expression of that love—"I'd kill for him"—both attracted and repelled me.

For a couple of days I did not know what to make of that meeting. I turned the incident over and over in my mind, replaying the conversation, looking for a handle. I did not know whether to dismiss the encounter as embarrassing or silly, a casual episode of real-life melodrama, or to treat it as a personal parable, a simple but profound mystery not meant to be completely understood.

I hesitated to mention the conversation to Lillian. I am more sentimental than she is; sometimes, I think, I stray into the zone of the maudlin. I was sure that I would not be able to recount the conversation without developing a catch in my throat. I expected that I would feel awkward in talking about it, even to Lillian.

DADDY'S HOME

Eventually, on an afternoon when Annie had a cold and I had rocked her to sleep, I found Lillian sitting in the study, and I tried to bring it up.

"You know, I was thinking: I hope we don't ever split up."

Lillian looked up at me, her expression locked between amusement and alarm. "What are you talking about?"

"I mean that if we ever separated, Annie would be a real problem. I wouldn't just hand her over, you know."

"I know that," Lillian said solemnly.

I paced the room in front of her chair while Lillian followed me with her eyes.

"I was just thinking about men who routinely hand over the children to their wives after a divorce," I said, "like it was carved in stone that kids go with their mothers. It's just crazy. But most men don't want them, I suppose."

I stopped pacing and turned to face Lillian. "I couldn't do that," I said.

"I know," she said again.

"I mean, I just feel too much for her to even imagine not being with her. Do you understand?"

Lillian smiled. "Yes, I think I do. You've spent almost two years earning that feeling."

I never did tell Lillian about the woman in the black coat. But as we began making plans to move, plans that would have me going to work and Lillian taking my place at home with Annie, I thought about that woman often. When I returned to the newsroom, spending at least ten hours a day away from home, was the responsibility for Annie the only thing I would give up? Or would I lose that feeling of closeness, that hard-earned understanding of love, too?

208

Chapter 18

Hot News and Cool

MIAMI WAS HOT. Miami is always hot in May; but the year we flew in from Michigan, the heat reflected more than just the Gulf Stream, the tropic breeze, and the migration of the sun. Miami was a city about to explode, and the heat was an index of combustion.

For a man who wanted to trade the calm of his two years at home with a baby for a daily fix of action, Miami was perfect. Within twelve months of my starting work as a general-assignment reporter for the *Miami Herald* in July 1979, the city would be threatened by a killer hurricane, rocked by three days of savage rioting, stunned by a record wave of murder, and inundated with one hundred and fifty thousand Caribbean refugees who quickly strained south Florida's diverse and delicate social fabric to the point of unraveling. In between these major crises, Miami was pockmarked by cocaine cowboy shoot-outs in suburban shopping centers, a police-brutality scandal, a run of airplane hijackings, and a tourist slump. Even the weather turned bad; in March 1980 the temperature on Miami Beach fell to an unprecedented thirty-two degrees.

No one could have predicted the turn in Miami's fortunes, but even a stranger like me could sense the imminence of calamity. It pressed in around us like the heat.

I was sitting on the rim of the L-shaped city desk, waiting to be taken to lunch and asked more questions about my journalistic experience and why I would like Miami. Looking across the room, through the glass walls that separated the executive editors' offices from the crowd of reporters, I had to squint against the glare of sunlight dancing off the water of Biscayne Bay. A formation of pelicans glided by the window, hugely close, looking like pterodactyls. They startled me. Lillian and Annie waited in a nearby hotel, probably in the swimming pool. I felt a long way from home.

In front of me on the desk lolled a dead sea of newspapers; telephone books; pens and nubs of pencils; snaking Teletype copy; overflowing ashtrays; Coke cans; cascades of carbon paper tumbling from In and Out baskets; notebooks and telephones. All of the telephones seemed to be ringing. The only other person at the desk was John Brecher, a thin, pale, fidgety assistant city editor whom I would come to know as a wise and careful craftsman with reporter's copy. I knew him then only as someone who appeared to be very different from me.

Brecher, wearing a white shirt and a loosened tie, was leaning back in his chair while browsing through the com-

Hot News and Cool

puter. As he punched buttons on a typewriter keyboard, words spilled out across a terminal's television screen. There were six computer terminals mounted on the city desk; three dozen others stared blankly down the length of the quiet newsroom. These video-display terminals were the first such tools of electronic journalism I had seen in operation, and my ignorance of them contributed to the low hum of apprehension I felt.

Suddenly, Brecher sat up straight in his chair. "Where did this hijacking come from?" he shouted.

A short, graying man seated at a terminal on a desk behind Brecher swiveled around to face us. "I just sent that into your queue," he said. "That was a Miami flight, and I think we had that guy before."

"This is the guy, the former Cuban air ace," said Brecher excitedly. "Christ!"

He peered intently into the screen, reading impatiently as the story rolled up from the bottom. "Where is everyone?" he said loudly, scanning the near-deserted newsroom. "Why are there never any reporters around here?" Exasperated, he answered his own question: "Because it's noon, and everyone's having a good lunch somewhere."

Brecher grabbed up a phone and punched out a number. He cradled the receiver in the crook of his neck, and turned to me. "This guy was a lieutenant in the Cuban Air Force. Ten years ago he flew his jet to Miami. Now he takes a Delta 707 to go back. He's running his own air-taxi service." Into the phone he asked, "Jenkins there?"

To me he said, "Damn. We've got a verdict due in a wonderful fatal-stabbing trial, eighteen special investigative projects going, and I can't find a reporter. This is going to be a hell of a good story, too."

My stomach flipped nervously; I feared he was going to ask me to handle the story. I had not written a hard news

211

story in three years. I had not been hired yet. I didn't know Miami. I wasn't ready.

"The Duke died, too," Brecher said.

"The duke?" I wondered aloud. The duke of Wellington? The duke of Earl? I didn't know *anything.*

"John Wayne," Brecher said in response to my incomprehension. "You know, the Duke."

"In Miami?"

"No," he laughed. "That's the only thing that didn't happen in Miami today."

He turned back to the terminal. "We'll get lunch in a few minutes," he said, shaking a cigarette out of a pack. "I tell you, Miami is a hell of a news town. The place is nuts." He paused, impatiently blowing smoke. "Where did you say you were from?"

Before I could answer, he spun back to face the terminal, his long fingers snapping down on the keys in a rapid-fire click. The phone was still wedged against his shoulder.

"Small town in central Michigan," I said, thinking of my own two-fingered typing technique as I watched Brecher's hands fly across the keyboard. "Fifty miles north of Lansing."

"Oh, yeah," he said absently, continuing to type. "Way up there in the middle of nowhere."

"Yeah," I said, in a tone as distracted as his. "Way up there."

Twenty minutes later I hurried to keep up with Brecher as we walked two blocks to a restaurant. The temperature was in the eighties, the humidity visible around the edges of my glasses. I mopped sweat from my face and loosened my tie.

"Is this typical?" I asked, meaning the heat.

"Oh, yeah, the place is crazy," said Brecher. "There isn't another city like it. Dope, violence, weirdos, hurricanes, the mix of cultures, tourists . . . some days we can hardly get it all into the paper."

"Sounds crazy," I said.

"Oh, it is," he said with undisguised relish. "It's bizarre. Are you fast? If you can write fast, put a story together in a hurry, that's a key thing."

"Yeah, I think so," I said, taking another swipe at my forehead with the handkerchief and wishing I were more confident. "But it's been a while."

If there was a theme running through my interviews with several *Miami Herald* editors over those two days in May, that was it: It's been a while.

"So," said one rangy, amiable editor, no older than I, as he scanned my résumé later that afternoon, "you've been in Michigan for—let's see, three years. And you've been free-lancing, is that right?"

"Right. While my wife was working at a small college, I was home with our infant daughter and doing some free-lancing."

"Hmmm. How was that?"

"Oh, it was a wonderful experience. I sure didn't know much about babies when I started, but now I think I got the hang—"

"No, I mean the free-lancing. Can you make any real money that way? You say here you sold to the *Free Press,* the *News, Baby Talk—Baby Talk?* Never heard of that one."

"It's a magazine for new parents. We used to get it free from the diaper service."

"What kind of money can they pay?" The editor scowled.

"Not much," I said, trying for a lighthearted laugh while wondering why I had bothered to mention the magazine in the résumé. "I think I got twenty-five dollars."

He shook his head. "Well, it's pretty fast-paced here," he

said, as if concerned that I did not fully appreciate just how big Miami was.

"I know," I said. "Miami is a great news town."

Ultimately, I was hired despite my two years of inexplicable deviance as a househusband. The editors of the *Miami Herald* decided to trust my experience as a reporter, my recommendations, and my scores on psychological tests, and, like most everyone else, simply ignore my venture into homemaking. Like me, they figured I was ready to get back to work.

We moved to Miami in July, when, in the heat and humidity, the backyards revert to jungle and the people stay indoors. For three weeks we lived in motel rooms, venturing out only to swim and eat and hunt for a house. On cool mornings I opened the balcony door to the rollicking aria of the mockingbird; in the afternoon I watched in awe as the towering blue-black thunderheads rolled in from the Everglades, booming and flashing. As I described our life in Miami in letters to family and friends, the days in Michigan seemed a peaceful, distant dream.

It is stupendously noisy here. Our motel room is right by the Dixie Highway, eight lanes of perpetual motion, and I am never sure if the humming in my ears is from the traffic, the air conditioner, or mosquitoes.

We spend most of our time running from our air-conditioned room to the air-conditioned car of our real-estate lady, who remains forever cheerful in the face of our thickening confusion. Buying a house is such an act of permanence, of commitment, of antisocialism. To say nothing of money. But we are a family now, not just a couple of vagabonds in a VW bus. Annie, I suppose, will need a neighborhood, schools, friends her age. We will need a

Hot News and Cool

place within tolerable commuting distance of downtown, a place with more than one bedroom, a watertight roof, a lawn. It all seems so foreign, and it tires me.

Annie has embraced our new surroundings with much more exuberance than Lil or I have had time to muster. She chases lizards through the palm fronds, and is a natural in the motel pool. We are still melting in the heat, and she has molted. She is a water baby. In a few weeks, I imagine, she will take up surfing, give up shoes, grow up Latin. In this sun, her hair will remain blond forever.

Annie, weeks away from her second birthday, was increasingly talkative, and, while unable to articulate the strangeness she saw around her, she did know her life had changed. She reacted by demanding more and more attention. Living on top of one another in one small room, our attention was easily gained. Climbing unassisted from her small rented crib in the corner of the room, Annie began each day by turning on the television, and turning up the volume. She treated our beds like trampolines, occasionally tumbling to the floor in surprise and tears. She bit holes in the tube of toothpaste, played in the toilet bowl, tore pages out of the Gideon Bible.

Eating out, once a pleasure, soon became a test of endurance or speed-eating. Annie's patience for sitting convivially at the table was limited. After pounding on a couple of packages of saltines, reducing them to dust in the tray of her high chair, and spilling her drink, she was often ready to leave before the food that Lillian and I had ordered had even arrived. We began to rely more and more on room service, or restaurants that promised to deliver fast food even faster.

Lillian and I knew about the stress of moving, of househunting, of starting a new job. We could anticipate the demands of change, and try to prepare. But Annie could not.

She knew only that her routine of the past two years had been abruptly abandoned. Through books, the experts reminded us that Annie was no longer a baby. She was, in the words of psychologist Burton L. White, "a relatively complete junior human being" who had constructed "an elaborate social contract with [her] primary caretaker." Unilaterally, I had violated that contract. At what cost? I wondered.

In trying to describe what she noticed, Annie began to form two-word sentences that often sounded like cryptograms.

"Katy no," she said, mystified over the disappearance of the dog, whom we had left temporarily with my parents in Ohio.

"No, Katydog is coming later in the airplane," I explained carefully. "She is coming."

Annie seemed to offer a commemorative sentence for each major disruption in her life. When, two weeks after our arrival in Miami, I began to work, she took note of my regular daylong absence. "Daddy work," she said, and in that expression I never failed to hear a note of betrayal.

Daddy worked. It exhausted me. Even during those first few days when I seemed to do nothing but fill out a few more employee forms or read the *Herald* style book, I came home about 7:30 in the evening ready for bed. The hours were too late in the day, the traffic was maddening, and my rhythm was all wrong. Sitting at my desk in the newsroom, surrounded by noise and people and the nervous tension of deadline after deadline, I realized how casual my pace at home had been, and how I had become attuned to it.

In those first weeks of being a reporter again, I worried that I had made a bad choice, that I was no longer equipped to function with speed, under the pressures of the clock, to write quickly on any subject, on demand.

Hot News and Cool

I also realized how quickly I grew away from my daughter, and lost track of her. While I was away at work, Lillian was busy making connections—with friends of friends at the University of Miami, with people in the career-counseling business, with other mothers of small children. She began laying the groundwork for what would become a bilingual cooperative preschool, and, through sheer doggedness, she involved herself and Annie in a network of friends of whom I knew nothing.

"What happened to your knee?" I asked Annie one evening as I wrestled her into her pajamas. She was wearing a kneecap-size bandage.

"Boo-boo," she said, all seriousness.

"How did that happen?"

"Fell down," she said.

"How did it happen?" I asked, enjoying her nascent ability to actually converse.

"Fell down," she earnestly repeated.

"At Joel's house," prompted Lillian.

"Joel's house," Annie echoed.

"Who is Joel?" I said, turning to Lillian.

"He's the three-year-old son of Carla Diaz, who is a friend of John Montgomery at the university, who is in the Psychology Department, and was at Kent State. And we're going to Joel's birthday party on Saturday. Right, Annie?"

"'lado," said Annie.

"Lado?" I did not understand.

"*Helado*—ice cream," explained Lillian.

"Spanish! She speaks Spanish?" I asked, incredulous.

"*Sí. ¿Cómo no? Estamos en Miami ahora,*" said Lillian.

New friends, new injuries, a new language: Already, it seemed, my daughter had turned into a stranger. While I was at work, she kept growing, learning, living. Perhaps I had spent too much time wondering how *she* would adjust

DADDY'S HOME

to our separation, and not enough time figuring out how *I* would handle the loss. Just as Annie had grown dependent on and accustomed to me for her primary care, I was used to having her on my hip, in my arms, nearby. I felt somehow naked without her, as if I had forgotten something. I missed the day full of opportunities to kiss her cheek, to nuzzle her neck. After all that time shepherding a helpless child from babyhood, I turned over to Lillian a companion.

"Just when she's getting to the age where she can hold up her end of the conversation, I leave," I said one night to Lillian while Annie slept peacefully in her motel crib. "Maybe I should have taken the second two years."

"Too late now," said Lillian. "Your turn to bring home a paycheck."

"How about if I put a by-line on her, so people will know I had a hand in getting her this far?" I asked with telling facetiousness. "I'm going to miss her."

"I know," said Lillian. "But we're not going anywhere. Just hang in there; you'll see you have the easy part."

Within a few weeks, after I had learned my way around the newsroom, made acquaintances, and had written several by-lined stories on deadline, I began to feel comfortable at work. I still missed the time I'd once had with Annie, but I also realized it was easier to be a reporter than it was to be a househusband, and I realized that most clearly at lunchtime. Between noon and one o'clock, I often joined colleagues for lunch, either in the *Herald*'s cafeteria or at a restaurant nearby. During those first few lunches, I had a nagging suspicion that I should be doing something; I couldn't seem to relax. Eventually, I realized that I was used to lunching with Annie. Besides helping her spoon in food, that meant occupying her with crackers, picking up morsels from the floor, wiping her face, steadying her drink, distracting her from fits of impatience or ill humor.

As a reporter, there was no one to look out for over lunch but me. I could relax, without fear that one of my companions at the table would start throwing SpaghettiOs or a tantrum. At home, I had discovered, a man's work was never done. But at work, I took breaks all day long, and I did not have to rock anyone to sleep to earn them.

As a reporter, I regained an identity that others could readily accept. When we opened a checking account, I did not have to explain that my wife won the bread, or exaggerate my free-lance earnings, or pretend that I was writing a novel. My job was enough for the whole family. "Oh, you work for the *Herald?*" a bank official would say, reading the card I had filled out. "A reporter? I'll have to watch for your name. And your wife . . ."

"Self-employed," I said.

"Fine," as if that were of absolutely no importance. "Now, do you want to apply for one of our bank credit cards?"

When I began work as a reporter, I got more than an approved identity and a paycheck, however. I also got a whole set of emotional baggage that I did not have before. I had never been a reporter *and* a father. And as I began to get pulled into the turbulent Miami vortex, I realized that I carried Annie with me everywhere. She was with me through the Miami riot.

"David! Damn, don't hit any of these kids on the street. That's about all it would take to get this riot started up again."

"Relax," David Walters told me. "I'm not going to hit anyone. You're the most nervous passenger I've ever had."

"Well . . ."

DADDY'S HOME

Well, I was nervous. Although the killing had stopped, the smoke from several fresh fires still cast an ugly pall over Liberty City, Miami's most desolate black ghetto. For three days, Walters and his colleagues on the *Herald*'s photographic staff had been tailgating police cars and drafting fire trucks to get frightening pictures of young men with rocks in their hands and police with guns drawn. They had earned their reputation for courage, and, once earned, they nourished it. Walters, for one, was not going to ease off now.

We skidded around a corner in pursuit of a truckload of National Guardsmen who had been ordered to protect fire fighters at the scene of a burning store. My stomach fluttered, and I hung on to my seat belt.

"At least we've got these press cards," I said, trying for a note of cool, dry humor. "We can use them for shields."

"Ha!" said Walters as he swerved to avoid a makeshift barricade in the street. "These things will make handy body tags—if they don't melt."

Whoa! I wanted to scream. What are we doing here? Forget all that social psychology about a man's need to reaffirm his masculinity in the arena of the workplace. I don't want to prove my manhood. I have a child. I am needed at home. I have other responsibilities, and this is dangerous. We could be hurt or killed out here!

Of course, I did not yell any such thing. I hung on and kept my mouth shut; and when we got to the fire, Walters began taking pictures while I collected the story from fire fighters and guardsmen and police officers and people on the street. What was burning? What did the scene look like? What did the people say?

Back in the newsroom, writing the story, I felt a satisfaction in having been there, in having done my job, in refusing to surrender to fears of personal disaster. I knew then that I had exaggerated the danger; but I also knew that that

Hot News and Cool

aggrandizement added to the exhilaration I felt. I did not contrive the chance for such exhilaration, but, after the fact, I responded to it, recognizing as a reporter the sort of emotional rush that is never available to the househusband.

Several months later, sitting in a darkened hotel room in Kingston, Jamaica, where I had been sent to await the arrival of hurricane Allen, the storm of the century, so I could report on its fury, I once again felt the same ambivalence I had sometimes known as a househusband reading the newspaper over breakfast. As the keening wind snapped power lines, and transformers blew up on the hillsides in showers of blue-white sparks, I lay on the bed and listened to Bob Marley and the Wailers on the radio, their lilting reggae comforting me with its familiarity. I wanted to be there in the path of a 170-mile-an-hour wind, wanted to cover that hurricane story; but at the same time, I felt I had so much to lose. That feeling, that weight, was new.

It was not just my life that was endangered, although I was certain it was; more than that, my life as a father was on the line. Annie made me more than just a man. Thinking about her, I wanted to be less careless, more circumspect. I wanted to weigh the chances I took for the sake of my career, or for Knight-Ridder, Incorporated, or for the people's right to know. I wanted to see my daughter again. I wanted to see who she would turn out to be.

A reporter's days of peril, real or imagined, are relatively few. I seem to spend most of my working life holding on to a telephone, hoping to hear the true ring of a good quote or the glint of information that could lead me to something more. In the course of my normal day as a reporter, I have time to think about what I do for a living, to ponder the future, to recall as halcyon all my days in Michigan when the world was smaller, and turned more slowly. I think often of Annie, and wonder what she and Lillian are doing. I miss

DADDY'S HOME

knowing her as intimately as I once did, and I miss keeping daily track of her development and discoveries. I miss being able to hug her at will.

Annie makes me vulnerable—to longing, to daydreams, to fears, to pain. She has also made me capable of a love that seems boundless. That lack of constraint sometimes scares me. I feel responsible for that love, and wary of its energy, but I have grown comfortable with its weight.

Annie has, finally, by making me a father, made me more of a man. As a househusband, I was forced to take stock of what I am, and what I think and believe, and what I want to do. While mixing my emotions, she has ordered my priorities, and irreversibly changed my life. She makes me proud.

Epilogue

IN *Black Like Me,* John Howard Griffin describes darkening his skin in order to travel through the Deep South as a black man because he believed "the only way to find out if we had second-class citizens and what their plight was, would be to become one of them." Once transformed from white to black, he wrote, "I prepared to walk into a life that appeared suddenly mysterious and frightening."

Never once in my two years as a househusband was I mistaken for a woman. Nor did I ever really feel feminine. Maybe it was the beard.

Of course, it was not my intention to pass as a woman. Neither did I set out, like a secret explorer, expressly to plumb the depths of female society, gauge discrimination against women, or find out, once and for all, what the phrase "just a housewife" really means. No. I spent two years at home because Lillian and I had the good fortune to have a child, and that child needed love and care. I was available and willing.

Nevertheless, there were times when the life I led did take on a mysterious, even frightening, air. The mystery swelled between diaper changes and tuna casseroles and trips to the doctor's office, confusing me about just *why* I was at home, the only househusband I knew. Mystery shrouded my child's sudden fever, her normal yet miraculous growth, her innate persistence that overnight turned her from a scuttling infant to an upright walker. Our mutual evolution, from awkward strangers to symbiosis, remains mysteriously sublime.

What occasionally frightened me as a father were reminders of how great was the responsibility I shouldered, how uncharted my course. Undoubtedly, the first years of a child's life were "extraordinarily important" in determining her later development, as psychologist Burton L. White emphasized in *A Parent's Guide to the First Three Years*. Of course the bond between the child and the parents was critical. But fathers remained pigs in a poke, strange animals in a nursery. "We have too little solid information to say much of anything definite about the importance of fathering," said White.

If there exists a near-universal taboo against men providing childcare, that taboo likely exists for a reason. But we broke it. At what cost? Would my daughter fall innocent victim to a well-intentioned but misplaced adventurism? Would our rash iconoclasm leave us with an emotionally confused child? How would our father-tended baby turn out?

Epilogue

Annie is now almost four. She is tall for her age, and lean. Although we keep expecting her hair to darken, she is still blond. At times she is headstrong; she is always physically active, curious, inquisitive, demanding. She has a vivid imagination, an affectionate nature, and a talent for incisive mimicry that occasionally allows Lillian and me to see ourselves.

I often see in Annie reminders of the way she was, when I knew her better. I remember the long bouts with colic, the problems with her eye, her pure delight at the moment she figured out how to spring off her toes in the Johnny Jump-Up seat from which she hung in the doorway. The chip in her front tooth recalls an afternoon on the front steps, when the older boy next door pushed her down onto the concrete walk. I sat there and watched. I can still see the blood trickle down her chin, and still feel the pull of anguish as her eyes welled and she turned to ask me why.

When the stump of her umbilical cord fell off, I was there, too. I considered saving it, pressing it into her scrapbook like a prom corsage. Had Lillian not convinced me that saving that bit of dead skin, no matter how symbolic, was excessive, it would be there today, along with so many photographs of the child that friends accused me of trying to compile a time-lapse record of her life.

For two years, keeping track of Annie, watching her carefully and charting her growth, was an important part of what I did each day. During that time, she was rarely far from my sight, and never out of my mind.

She is much more complex now, and, even if I were not working away from home, keeping track of her development would not be as easy as it was. I am not sure how she learned to buckle her sandals, but she can. She can write her name, recognize the letters of the alphabet, count to twenty, and dress herself. She has learned how to dribble a basketball. When I feed her soft setups, she hits a solid forehand with an oversize tennis racket. She runs with a smooth grace.

Five mornings a week she goes to the cooperative bilingual nursery school founded by her mother, where she paints with impressionistic abandon, swings upside down from the monkey bars, engages in elaborate make-believe games with her friends, and learns songs in Spanish.

Recently, Annie has taken to wearing dresses in imitation of her mother, who is pregnant with our second child and has temporarily given up shorts and slacks in favor of looser garb. But with her hair cut short for the summer, Annie in anything but a dress is sometimes mistaken for a boy— especially, it seems, when she is with me.

"Hi there, big boy," a gas station attendant said to her the other day as he peered into the back seat. "Having fun with your dad?"

Bemused, Annie smiled knowingly when he walked away. "I'm not a boy, I'm a *girl*," she said to me. She shook her head over the attendant's ignorance. "Silly," she said.

Annie is not androgynous. She identifies with her mother, and with other girls. She plays house. Her favorite toys are dolls. She recently told Lillian, "Ladies don't work."

I received that report with surprise. I appreciate the irony of that observation from a child whose parents put so much stock in nonsexist childrearing, and who try to avoid stereotypes. But practically, realistically, what other conclusion might Annie come to? For the past two years, I have been the breadwinner. Although Lillian has continued to work, counseling clients in the living room, leaving for weekends to conduct seminars on career changing, daddy is the one Annie sees leave for work each morning, the one she sees come home late for dinner. Among our friends, many women do work. But at the nursery school, the parent who

Epilogue

puts in the morning as teacher is invariably a mother. In the world that Annie regularly sees, the men are away at work and the women are with the children.

The arrival of our second child signals a change for all of us. Annie is filled with wonder over the prospect of becoming a sister. She plans to help care for the baby, to soothe her sibling's cries. Lillian chafes under the restraints of part-time work, the stress of full-time childcare. I understand. I have been glutted with deadline news and the demands of the daily schedule.

Just as Griffin learned about the lives of blacks in the South, I think my two years at home taught me about the lives of women who work as housewives and mothers. At home with Annie and the laundry and the shopping and the cooking, nurturing her along with the subtle satisfactions of being a parent, I gained an appreciation of the life that millions of women lead—and the life that millions of women are giving up. Being a housespouse, like being a newspaper reporter, is a confusion of joy and frustration.

Back at work, my ability to identify with mothers and housewives often makes me uncomfortable. I am impatient, for example, when a male colleague grumbles about the demands of a journalist's job, bemoans the lack of time he has for his family, and then heads out after work for a drink to ease his burden. "But what about your wife at home?" I am tempted to demand, full of righteous indignation at his insensitivity to the domestic hardships I so well know. "Can't you understand what a tough, trying day she has probably put in? Don't you think you should go home and help out?"

More than ever, I am intolerant of sexist jokes, offended by the scarcity of women in management positions at the newspaper, annoyed when I see evidence of how the Old Boys' Network keeps working for men at women's expense.

DADDY'S HOME

Occasionally I hear comments about children or roles or responsibilities that remind me that most men, and many women, see behavior as prescribed by gender, and that reminder not only exasperates me but makes me realize what an outsider I remain, even back in the office.

I have been asked by male and female colleagues how I could have given up the quick pace, the professional status, or the paycheck to stay home with a baby. "Easy," I answered, glibly offhand. "I wanted a change. Even the news seems to get old after a while."

No one has ever asked me how I could have given up the life of a househusband to resume my career as a journalist. That question must seem pointless, the answer self-evident. To many people a reporter's life appears full of daily adventure, excitement, novelty. Reporters are acquainted with the important, or the influential, or are on the scene of history. They are paid to be creative and resourceful; they get their names in the paper, and public credit. Wondering why a man would choose to trade his diaper bag and apron for a notebook and a press card is like wondering why a furry caterpillar longs to become a butterfly. It's only natural.

Why then, just weeks after being issued a press card, being pointed to a desk, and assigned to write ten inches of copy on a dump-truck-drivers' strike, did I wonder if I had made a mistake? Didn't I want out of the house? Didn't I want to become involved again in current events, rejoin the world, draw a paycheck, feel like a professional, wear business clothes, have a *career?* Why, as the clock ticked away toward deadline and the electric typewriter insistently hummed, did I sit wondering if Annie needed a vitamin supplement?

Ah, ambivalence. Were those deathless afternoons with an irritable baby really longer than a day spent sitting through a commission hearing so boring and so uneventful

Epilogue

that not even Damon Runyon could have written a story about it with enough life to get into the paper? Were the frustrations of unreachable sources, make-work assignments, and impossible deadlines really worse than those that mushroomed up on a hot afternoon with a cantankerous child?

Back in the newsroom, I had regrets. I did want to work as a reporter again, but I did not want to give up my child in order to do it. I wanted everything. I wanted to be a journalist *and* a full-time father. I did not want to miss a single good story, and I did not want to miss Annie's smallest advance. I wanted it all.

Before the birth of my first child, I thought of Thoreau's explanation for moving to Walden Pond: "I went to the woods because I wished to live deliberately, to front only the essential facts of life, and see if I could not learn what it had to teach, and not, when I came to die, discover that I had not lived." After Annie's birth, I wanted to be there, to examine her life and mine, to learn, like Thoreau, through experience if our existence be either mean or sublime. I did not want to discover one day that my child had completed her infancy and that I had missed it.

Now, with another child coming, I hear the same call. I am drawn by the same invitation, struck by the same imperative. Perhaps it is unnecessary to repeat the experience of being a househusband to learn about life at home with a baby; it is both mean and sublime, I know. But this child will be like no other. Do I dare miss that infancy?

From my desk in the newsroom I can look out a far window onto Biscayne Bay. Along a causeway crossing the water, people fish. Sunlight glints off the metal eyes of the fishing rods. Cars speed by, boats pass under the saluting drawbridge, and the pastel scene shimmers in silence, unreal and hypnotic.

On many afternoons I get telephone calls from Annie.

DADDY'S HOME

She asks me when I am going to be home. She tells me what she did in nursery school. "I miss you," she says in closing; and although I am never sure she comprehends the concept of longing and separation, I am always moved.

Near the bridgetender's tower, a least tern plummets headfirst into the water, a brilliant white falling star, and then flutters upward on skittering wings. From my distant vantage, I cannot see whether or not the bird has been successful in its dive for food. I daydream. I think about the baby, tucked in Lillian's belly. I visualize the birth, and then imagine the homecoming, and Annie's excitement. I see myself, the childstruck father, searching the face of a newborn who lies lightly in my arms. I look for clues. Could those first two years ever again be so mysterious, so frightening, so full of wonder?